POEMS
of
PRAYER

Prayer is a conversation with God.

Clement of Alexandria

Song is the leap of mind in the eternal breaking out into sound.

St. Thomas Aquinas

Surely there was a time I might have trod
The sunlit heights, and from life's dissonance
struck one clear chord to reach the ears of God.

Oscar Wilde

The poet to himself must sing
When none but God is listening.

John Banister Tabb

Because the road was steep and long
And through a dark and lonely land,
God set upon my lips a song
And put a lantern in my hand.

Joyce Kilmer

Prayer is a trap-door out of sin.
Prayer is a mystic entering in
To secret places full of light.
It is a passage through the night.

Jessica Powers

POEMS OF PRAYER

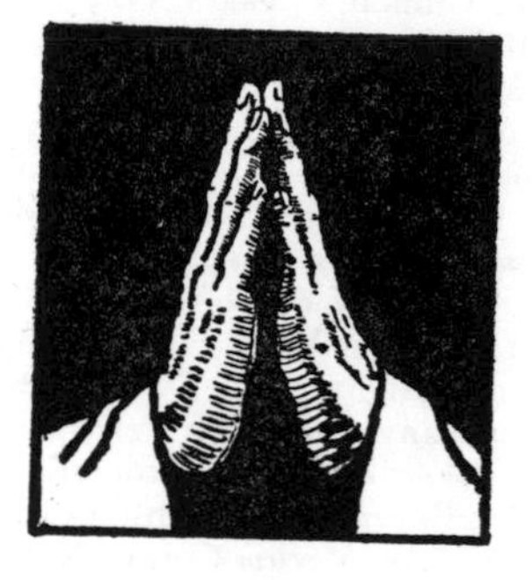

compiled and edited
by
RALPH L. WOODS

Hawthorn Books, Inc. *Publishers* New York

 All inquiries should be addressed to Hawthorn Books, Inc., 70 Fifth Avenue, New York City 11. This book was manufactured in the United States of America and published simultaneously in Canada by McClelland & Stewart, Ltd., 25 Hollinger Road, Toronto 16. Library of Congress Catalogue Number: 62-10888. Suggested Decimal Classification 808.1.

FIRST EDITION

May, 1962

ACKNOWLEDGMENTS

Grateful acknowledgment is made to the following copyright owners for permission to reprint the poems specified:

America Press, for James E. Tobin's "Ballade of a Voice Crying"; Rev. Alfred Barrett's, S.J., "Chant of Departure" and "Unearth"; Ellen Gilbert's "Prodigal"; Helen R. Kahn's "Confession"; Florence Gilmore's "God's Way"; Ruth Mary Fox's "Prayer" and "Petition"; Sister Miriam's, R.S.M., "Prayer Against Alien Rest"; Sister Mary Davida's "Swimmer's Prayer"; Sister Mary Paulinus' "Canticle of Weakness"; Isabel C. Clarke's "In Humbleness"; Eleanor M. Leary's "Thanks Given," reprinted by permission of AMERICA, *National Catholic Weekly Review*, 920 Broadway, New York 10, N.Y.

Benziger Brothers, Inc., for a passage from *"Dies Irae"* as translated in *The Sunday Missal*, by Rev. F. X. Lasance, edition of 1940.

Miss Jo Bingham, for her "Prayer for a New House."

Katherine Brégy for her "Playing With Fire," "Offertory," and "A Little While," from her *Ladders and Bridges*, copyright, 1936, David McKay Co.

The Bruce Publishing Company, for Helen Parry Eden's "His Hic Alienigena" and "Post-Communion" from her *Poems and Verses*, copyright, 1942, by Helen Parry Eden.

Burns and Oates, Ltd., for Robert Hugh Benson's "At High Mass," "Lines," "Contrition," "Wedding Hymn," and *"Ave Verum Corpus Natum,"* from his *Poems*, 1914.

Chatto and Windus, Ltd., for eight poems from *The Poem Book of the Gael*, translations by Eleanor Hull and Douglas Hyde, 1912.

Fray Angelico Chavez for his "Prayer for the Nations" from his *Eleven Lady Lyrics and Other Poems*, published by St. Anthony Guild Press, copyright, 1945, by Fray Angelico Chavez.

Chilton Company—Book Division, for "Prayer That an Infant May Not Die" by Francis Jammes, translated by Joseph T. Shipley, published in *Modern French Poetry*, copyright, 1926, 1954, by Greenberg, Publishers.

The Devin-Adair Co., for Hugh Francis Blunt's "An Offering" and "My God," from his *Songs for Sinners*, copyright, 1912, 1940, by The Devin-Adair Co.

Dodd, Mead and Co., for 8 lines from G. K. Chesterton's "Hymn for the Church Militant" and all of "Hymn," both in *Collected Poems of G. K. Chesterton*, copyright, 1932, by Dodd, Mead and Co., reprinted by permission of the Estate of Canon Percy Dearmer.

Doubleday and Co. Inc. for "Prayer for a Soldier in France," from *Poems, Essays and Letters* by Joyce Kilmer, copyright, 1918, by Geo. H. Doran Co.; and four lines from "Love's Lantern" from Joyce Kilmer's *Trees and Other Poems*, copyright, 1914, by Geo. H. Doran Co., both reprinted by permission of Doubleday and Co. Inc.; "Vigils" from *Vigils* by Aline Kilmer, copyright, 1921, by Geo. H. Doran and Co. reprinted by permission of Doubleday and Co.; "Candles That Burn" from *Candles That Burn* by Aline Kilmer, copyright, 1919, by Geo. H. Doran and Co., reprinted by permission of Doubleday and Co. Inc.

The Downside [Benedictine] Abbey, England, for "Hymn to Our Lady" by Dom Bede Camm, O.S.B.

Rev. William Noé Field for his "Psalm for Orders," "For an Ordinand," "Lady of the Lilacs," "Make of My Soul, O Lord," from his *Hear My Heart,* copyright, 1951, by Washington Irving Publishing Company.

Harcourt, Brace and World, Inc., for T. A. Daly's "The Man's Prayer" from *Selected Poems,* by T. A. Daly, copyright, 1936, by Harcourt, Brace and World, Inc., and reprinted with their permission.

Howard Hart for his "Holy Infant of Good Health."

Bruce Humphries, Publishers, for "On the Day the Holy *Viaticum* Came to Me," by Giovanni Prati, translated by Florence Trail and included in her *An Italian Anthology,* copyright, 1926, by Richard G. Badger.

The Hutchinson Publishing Group (Messrs. Rich and Cowan Ltd.), for Lord Alfred Douglas' "A Prayer" from his *Collected Poems,* 1919.

Victoria Saffelle Johnson for her "Dedication."

Joseph Joel Keith for his "Immaculate Palms" which first appeared in *I Sing of a Maiden,* ed. by Sister M. Thérèse, copyright, 1947, by The Macmillan Co.

Blanche Mary Kelly for her "The Housewife's Prayer" and "The Mirror."

P. J. Kennedy and Sons, for a prose quotation and Psalm No. 8 from A. M. Sullivan's *Psalms of the Prodigal,* copyright, 1954, by A. M. Sullivan, published by P. J. Kennedy and Sons.

J. B. Lippincott Co., for "Dedication" by Victoria Saffelle Johnson, first published in *The Golden Book of Catholic Poetry,* ed. by Alfred Noyes, copyright, 1946, by J. B. Lippincott Co.

The Macmillan Co., for "Holy Communion in a Hospital" from Sister M. Madeleva's *Four Last Things,* copyright, 1953, by The Macmillan Co.; "As One Finding Peace," Part Five of "The King's Secret," from *The Collected Poems of Sister M. Madeleva,* copyright, 1927, by Sister M. Madeleva, 1947, by The Macmillan Co.; "Our Lady of the Refugees," "Before Perpetual Vows" and "Blessing of the Holy Family," from Sister Mary Maura's *Initiate the Heart,* copyright, 1946, by The Macmillan Co.; "Beautiful, O Love, Thou Art" and "O, with a gesture light," from Mary Dixon Thayer's *Songs Before the Blessed Sacrament,* copyright, 1932, by The Macmillan Co.; "Finding You" from Mary Dixon Thayer's *The Child on His Knees,* copyright, 1926, by The Macmillan Co.; all reprinted with permission of The Macmillan Co.

Harold Matson Company, for "The Prophet Lost in the Hills at Evening," by Hilaire Belloc from his *Sonnets and Verses,* published by Sheed and Ward, Inc.

Mother Mary Consolatrice, B.V.M., Superior General, Sisters of Charity of the Blessed Virgin Mary, for Sister Angelita's "An Evening Prayer" from her *Starshine and Candlelight,* copyright, 1925, 1953, by Appleton-Century Co.

A. R. Mowbray and Co. Ltd., for "Lord, Fill Me With Thy Love," by Father Andrew, S.D.C., from his *Collected Poems.*

Mrs. Sylvia Mulvey, for Alice Meynell's "The Unknown God," and "I Am the Way" from *The Poems of Alice Meynell,* 1940.

Oxford University Press, London, for Canon George Wallace Brigg's "I Knew Thee Not, Thou Wounded Son of God," from *Songs of Faith.*

Priests of the Holy Cross, Indiana Province, Notre Dame, Indiana, for "Holy Communion" by Rev. Speer Straham.

The Queen's Work, St. Louis, Mo., for three poems from *The World and the Waters* by Rev. Edward F. Garesche, S.J., copyright, 1918, 1946, by The Queen's Work.

John Jerome Rooney, for "St. Michael" and "Pentecostal Hymn" by John Jerome Rooney, Senior, from *Collected Poems,* copyright, 1938, by Marie Collins Rooney.

Sheed and Ward, Inc., for "Joseph of Dreams" from *Frost For St. Brigid,* by Sister Maris Stella, copyright, 1949, by Sheed and Ward, Inc., New York; nine lines from *The Complete Works of St. Teresa of Jesus,* vol. 3, translated and edited by E. Allison Peers, from the critical edition of P. Silverio de Santa Teresa, C.D., published in three volumes by Sheed and Ward, Inc., New York; "Immolation" from *Thronging Feet* by Robert Farren, published by Sheed and Ward, Inc., New York.

Mrs. Annie E. Shillito, England, for Rev. Edward Shillito's "Jesus of the Scars."
Sister Miriam, R.S.M. of the College Misericordia, Dallas, Pa., for her "I Pray for One I Love" in her *Woven of the Sky*, copyright, 1940, The Macmillan Co.
Sister Miriam of the Holy Spirit, D.C., Prioress of Carmelite Monastery, Wisconsin, for "To the Holy Ghost" and "Patron of the Church," from *The Place of Splendor* by Jessica Powers, copyright, 1946, by Cosmopolitan Science and Art Service Co. Inc.
The Society of Authors, London, England, and Miss Pamela Hinkson, for Katharine Tynan Hinkson's "The Man of the House," "Lux in Tenebris" and "Distraction."
Spirit and The Catholic Poetry Society of America, for the following from *Spirit, A Magazine of Poetry*: "Wall Crucifix" by John Duffy, C.Ss.R., "Grace for a Spring Morning," "Prayer at a Nursery Window" and "Wedding Hymn" by Frances Stoakley Lankford; "Reluctant Prodigal" by Ernestine Parsons; "Mary of Fatima: A Sequence" by Virginia Earle; "With Frankincense and Myrrh" by Jennie M. Palen; "Against Despair" by Sister Mary Ada, C.S.J.; "Contentment" by Jacqueline Noble; "Grace Before Planting in Wartime" by James L. Duff; "Cry from the Battlefield" by Robert Menth; "For Having Thee" by Francis X. Connolly.
A. M. Sullivan for his "A Prayer."
Rev. Francis Beauchesne Thornton for his "Flosculus Immortalis" from his *On Wings of Song*, Wanderer Press, copyright, 1928, 1956.
University of Notre Dame Press, for Rev. Charles L. O'Donnell's "Security," "Prayer for a Traveler," "Process," and "Resolution," all from *Collected Poems of Charles L. O'Donnell*, copyright, 1942, by University of Notre Dame Press.
A. P. Watt and Son, Miss D. E. Collins and Metheun and Co., Ltd., for 8 lines from G. K. Chesterton's "Hymn for the Church Militant" and all of "Hymn," from *Collected Poems of G. K. Chesterton*, reprinted by permission of Estate of Canon Percy Dearmer.
Clifford J. Laube, for his "Prayer of Perseverance."

In the case of several poems, diligent search has thus far failed to locate the possible copyright owners. Appropriate acknowledgments will be made in subsequent printings should such information be called to the editor's notice.

INTRODUCTION

Although a book titled *Poems of Prayer* needs no explanation, nevertheless a few comments and observations would seem appropriate and may be helpful.

When we remember that prayer is a lifting of the heart and mind to God—a conversation with God—and when we recognize that the mystery of God fills one with awe, then do we realize that poetry beautifully lends itself to prayer. For, in the words of Edwin Arlington Robinson, "Poetry tells us something that cannot be said." Thus poetry is a means by which the inexpressible may be communicated to the Incomprehensible.

The relationship between poetry and prayer is well stated by A. M. Sullivan, a contemporary American poet of recognized stature. In the introduction to his fine *Psalms of the Prodigial* Mr. Sullivan points out that "Poetry is essentially a spiritual enterprise even when it evokes the god of the natural order or challenges the god of the supernatural. . . . Poets who quarrel with God have a difficult time getting along without Him. . . . Shelley, a professed atheist, might state his lack of belief in prose, he couldn't demonstrate it in poetry. . . . Actually, there are few atheists among poets. . . . All prayer is poetry, but not all poetry is prayer."

Even those who do not customarily enrich their lives with poetry will appreciate from the preceding that one engaged in compiling a book such as this has a vast store of riches upon which to draw.

However, I have carefully limited the book's contents to poems that are unmistakeably prayers—poems wherein the minds and hearts are lifted in conversation with God; poems addressed only to God and to His Saints as intercessors. This ruled out hundreds of genuinely religious poems that have only an incidental prayer content, and those which end with a prayer after much expository content. In other words, the poems included in this volume are *wholly and exclusively poems of prayer.*

Moreover, although metaphysical poets are generously represented in these pages, I have nevertheless avoided obscure and complex poems no matter how beautiful and profound. The intellectual effort required to understand difficult metaphysical poetry would often deflect those who turn to the volume for devotional reading. Consequently, the poems in this collection are so clear and so appealing that the reader will often—perhaps usually—instinctively join the poet in his prayer.

It will immediately be noticed that this is primarily a volume of

Catholic prayer poems, written by Catholics. A few of the poems are by poets who later left the Church, but the poems of course remain as Catholic as when written. There are a larger number of truly beautiful poems written by those who are not Catholics, but which breathe a Catholic spirit, embrace a Catholic concept or speak eloquently to God in a spirit common to all who believe in Him.

I have been chiefly concerned that the poems selected be consistent with an essentially Catholic volume. But I have not permitted a poet's lack of orthodoxy to eliminate a poem of prayer that is obviously in the Catholic tradition or based on the considerable residues of Catholicism found in other Christian persuasions. In brief, I have considered the poem rather than the poet.

—RALPH L. WOODS

TABLE OF CONTENTS

LOVE: GOD'S LOVE FOR MAN, MAN'S LOVE OF GOD

SUBMISSION TO GOD

FAITH: PLEDGES AND PLEAS

FOR GRACE

FOR LIGHT AND GUIDANCE

PENITENCE AND PARDON

TO JESUS IN THE BLESSED SACRAMENT

BEFORE AND AFTER HOLY COMMUNION

MORNING PRAYER-POEMS

EVENING PRAYER-POEMS

THANKSGIVING AND GRATITUDE

DEDICATION

FOR PROTECTION AND PEACE

FOR THE HOME AND FAMILY

FOR SPECIAL PURPOSES, OCCASIONS, AND PEOPLE

FOR MERCY

THE LAST DAYS AND AFTER

POEMS OF PRAYER ESPECIALLY FOR CHILDREN

ADORATION AND PRAISE

"MY HEART IS READY, O GOD"

My heart is ready, O God, my heart is ready: I will sing, and will give praise, with my glory.
Arise, my glory; arise, psaltery and harp: I will arise in the morning early.
I will praise thee, O Lord, among the people, and I will sing unto thee among the nations.
For thy mercy is great above the heavens: and thy truth even unto the clouds.
Be thou exalted, O God, above the heavens, and thy glory over all the earth: that thy beloved may be delivered.

Psalm 107:2–7

"O FATHER, WE APPROACH THY THRONE"

O Father, we approach Thy throne,
Who bidst the glorious sun arise,
All-good, almighty and all-wise
Great Source of all things, God alone!

We see Thee, brighter than the rays
Of the bright sun, we see Thee shine!
As in a fountain, light divine,
We see Thee, endless fount of days!

We see Thee who our frame hast wrought
With one swift word from senseless clay;
Waked with one glance of heavenly ray
Our never dying souls from naught.

Those souls Thou lightest with the spark
At Thy pure fire; and gracious still,
Gav'st immortality, free-will,
And language not involved in dark!

Joost van den Vondel (translated by Sir John Bowring)

GOD

I see Thee in the distant blue;
But in the violet's dell of dew,
Behold, I *breathe and touch* Thee too.

John Banister Tabb

MY GOD, HOW WONDERFUL THOU ART

My God, how wonderful Thou art,
Thy majesty how bright,
How beautiful Thy mercy-seat,
In depths of burning light!

How dread are Thine eternal years,
O everlasting Lord;
By prostrate spirits day and night
Incessantly adored!

How wonderful, how beautiful,
The sight of Thee must be,
Thine endless wisdom, boundless power,
And awful purity!

O how I fear Thee, living God,
With deepest, tenderest fears,
And worship Thee with trembling hope,
And penitential tears!

Yet may I love Thee too, O Lord,
Almighty as Thou art,
For Thou hast stooped to ask me
The love of my poor heart.

Frederick W. Faber

THE SONG OF THE CREATURES

O most high, almighty, good Lord God, to Thee belong praise, glory, honor and all blessing!

Praised be my Lord God with all His creatures, and especially our brother the sun, who brings us the day and who brings us the light; fair is he and shines with very great splendor; O Lord, he signifies to us Thee!

Praised be my Lord for our sister the moon, and for the stars, the which He has set clear and lovely in heaven.

Praised be my Lord for our brother the wind, and for air and cloud, calms and all weather by which Thou upholdest life in all creatures.

Praised be my Lord for all those who pardon one another, and for His love's sake, and who endure weakness and tribulation; blessèd are they who peaceably shall endure. For Thou, O Most Highest, shalt give them a crown!

Praised be my Lord for our sister, the death of the body, from which no man escapeth. Woe to him who dieth in mortal sin! Blessèd are they who are found walking by Thy most holy will, for the second death shall have no power to do them harm.

Praise ye and bless the Lord, and give thanks unto Him and serve Him with great humility.

St. Francis of Assisi (translated by Matthew Arnold)

"GREAT ART THOU O GOD"

Great art Thou, O Lord, and greatly to be praised;
Great is Thy power, and of Thy wisdom there is no end.
And man, being a part of Thy creation, desires to praise Thee,—
Man who bears about with him his mortality,
The witness of his sin, even the witness that Thou "resistest the proud,"—
Yet man, this part of Thy creation, desires to praise Thee.
Thou movest us to delight in praising Thee;
For Thou hast formed us for Thyself,
And our hearts are restless till they find rest in Thee.

St. Augustine

THE ETERNAL FATHER

Father! the sweetest, dearest name,
That men or angels know!
Fountain of life, that had no fount
From which itself could flow!

Thy life is one unwearing day;
Before its "now" thou hast
No varied future yet unlived,
No lapse of changeless past.

Thou comest not, Thou goest not;
Thou wert not, wilt not be;
Eternity is but a thought
By which we think of Thee.

Frederick W. Faber

THY KINGDOM COME

Thou hope of all the lowly!
To thirsting souls how kind!
Gracious to all who seek Thee,
Oh, what to those who find!

My tongue but lisps Thy praises,
Yet praise me my employ;
Love makes me bold to praise Thee,
For Thou art all my joy.

In Thee my soul delighting,
Findeth her only rest;
And so in Thee confiding,
May all the world be blest!

Dwell with us, and our darkness
Will flee before Thy light;
Scatter the world's deep midnight,
And fill it with delight.

O all mankind! behold Him
And seek His love to know;
And let your hearts, in seeking,
Be fired with love and glow!

O come, O come, great Monarch,
Eternal glory Thine;
The longing world waits for Thee!
Arise, arise and shine!

St. Bernard of Clairvaux

ADORATION

I love my God, but with no love of mine,
For I have none to give;
I love thee, Lord, but all that love is thine
For by thy life I live.

I am as nothing, and rejoice to be
Emptied and lost and swallowed up in thee.

Thou Lord, alone, art all thy children need
And there is none beside;
From thee the streams of blessedness proceed;
In thee the blest abide,
Fountain of life and all-abounding grace,
Our source, our center and our dwelling place!

Madame Guyon

THE DIVINE PRESENCE

All but unutterable Name!
Adorable, yet awful sound!
Thee can the sinful nations frame
Save with their foreheads on the ground?

Soul-searching and all-cleansing Fire;
To see Thy countenance were to die:
Yet how beyond the bound retire
Of Thy serene immensity?

Thou mov'st beside us, if the spot
We change—a noteless, wandering tribe;
The orbits of our life and thought
In Thee their little arcs describe.

In their dead calm, at cool of day,
We hear Thy voice, and turn, and flee:
Thy love outstrips us on our way!
From Thee, O God, we fly—To Thee.

Aubrey Thomas de Vere

MY GOD

Mighty God they name Thee,
God Omnipotent;

Ruler they acclaim Thee
  Of the world's extent;
Yea, but I, a lowly clod,
Call Thee this—*My* God.

King of Heaven they bless Thee,
  King eternally;
God they do confess Thee
  Of infinity;
Yea, but I, the lowliest clod,
Call Thee this—*My* God.

Hugh Francis Blunt

AN ANCIENT IRISH HYMN

I offer Thee—
Every flower that ever grew,
Every bird that ever flew,
Every wind that ever blew,
  Good God!
Every thunder rolling,
Every church bell tolling,
Every leaf and sod.
  Laudamus Te!

I offer Thee—
Every wave that ever moved,
Every heart that ever loved,
Thee, Thy Father's Well-Beloved,
  Dear Lord!
Every river dashing,
Every lightning flashing,
Like an angel's sword,
  Benedicimus Te!

I offer Thee—
Every cloud that ever swept
O'er the skies, and broke and wept

In rain, and with the flow'rets slept,
My King!
Each communicant praying,
Every angel staying
Before Thy throne to sing!
Adoramus Te!

I offer Thee—
Every flake of virgin snow,
Every spring the earth below,
Every human joy and woe.
My Love!
O Lord! And all Thy glorious
Self, o'er death victorious,
Throned in heaven above.
Glorificamus Te!

Anonymous

A THANKSGIVING

Lord, in this dust Thy sovereign voice
First quicken'd love divine;
I am all Thine,—Thy care and choice,
My very praise is Thine.

I praise Thee, while Thy providence
In childhood frail I trace,
For blessings given, ere dawning sense
Could seek or scan Thy grace; . . .

Yet, Lord, in memory's fondest place
I shrine those seasons sad
When, looking up, I saw Thy face
In kind austereness clad. . . .

And such Thy tender force be still,
When self would swerve or stray,
Shaping to truth the froward will
Along Thy narrow way.

Deny me wealth, fear, far remove
  The love of power or name;
Hope thrives in straits, in weakness love,
  And faith in the world's shame.

John Henry Newman

A PRAYER

Be Thou my vision, O Lord of my heart,
Naught is all else to me, save that Thou art.

Thou my best thought by day and by night,
Waking or sleeping, Thy presence my light.

Be Thou my wisdom, Thou my true word;
I ever with Thee, Thou with me, Lord.

Thou my great father, I Thy dear son;
Thou in me dwelling, I with Thee one.

Be Thou my battle-shield, sword for the fight,
Be Thou my dignity, Thou my delight.

Thou my soul's shelter, Thou my high tower;
Raise Thou me heavenward, power of my power.

Riches I heed not, nor man's empty praise,
Thou mine inheritance now and always.

Thou, and Thou only, first in my heart,
High king of heaven, my treasure Thou art.

King of the seven heavens, grant me for dole,
Thy love in my heart, Thy light in my soul.

Thy light from my soul, Thy love from my heart,
King of the seven heavens, may they never depart.

With the high king of heaven, after victory won,
May I reach heaven's joys, O bright heaven's sun!

Heart of my own heart, whatever befall,
Still be my vision, O Ruler of all.

Anonymous (translated by Eleanor Hull from the 8th Century Gaelic)

From THE SHEPHERD'S HYMN

We saw Thee in Thy balmy nest,
Young dawn of our eternal Day;
We saw Thine eyes break from their East,
And chase the trembling shades away:
We saw Thee: and we blessed the sight,
We saw Thee by Thine own sweet light.

Welcome, all wonders in one sight!
Eternity shut in a span!
Summer in Winter, Day in Night!
Heaven in Earth, and God in Man!
Great little One! whose all-embracing birth
Lifts Earth to Heaven, stoops Heaven to Earth.

To Thee, meek Majesty, soft King
Of simple graces and sweet Loves:
Each of us his lamb will bring,
Each his pair of silver doves:
Till burnt at last in fire of Thy fair eyes,
Ourselves become our own best sacrifice!

Richard Crashaw

"GREAT KING, FROM HEAVEN'S HIGH THRONE DESCENDING LOW"

Great King, from heaven's high throne descending low,
In Bethlehem's stable born in cold and woe,
Thou shiverest in a manger, Babe Divine,
Much hast Thou borne for sin: how much for mine!

St. Alphonsus Liguori (translated by F. Husenbeth)

THE EPIPHANY

Look up, sweet Babe, look up and see
For love of Thee
Thus far from home
The east is come
To seek herself in Thy sweet eyes;
We, who strangely went astray,
Lost in a bright
Meridian night,
A darkness made of too much day,
Beckon'd from far
By Thy fair star,
Lo at last have found our way.

Richard Crashaw

"SHEPHERD OF EAGER YOUTH"

Shepherd of eager youth,
Guiding in love and truth
Through devious ways;
Christ, our triumphant King,
We come Thy name to sing,
And here our children bring,
To sound Thy praise.

Thou art our Holy Lord,
The all-subduing Word,
Healer of strife;
Thou didst Thyself abase,
That from sin's deep disgrace
Thou mightest save our race,
And give us life.

Ever be Thou our Guide,
Our Shepherd and our Pride,
Our Staff and Song;
Jesus, Thou Christ of God,

By Thy enduring word,
Lead us where Thou hast trod,
Make our faith strong.

Clement of Alexandria (translated by Henry M. Dexter)

CHRISTMAS GREETING

Good morning, Lord! For little boys
The Day more generous to joys
Than unto men, they say;
If so, for greater happiness
Teach us Thy holy name to bless
With fuller hearts than they.

John Banister Tabb

FROM THE LATIN OF ST. BERNARD

Jesu, how sweet the memory
That fills my soul with thoughts of Thee!
But sweeter far Thou art to me,
When bowed before Thee tremblingly.

Never hath poesy been found
To utter word with sweeter sound
Than Thy dear name, sweet Jesu bound,
And pierced for us with many a wound!

Jesu, the hope of those who sigh,
Jesu, who hear'st the mourner's cry;
How good to those that to'ards thee fly,
But what to those who dwell on high! . . .

Jesu, our only thought then be;
Jesu, our hope in misery;
Oh! may we soon, dissolved in Thee,
Thy praises sing eternally!

J. J. Callanan

"JESUS, THE VERY THOUGHT OF THEE"

Jesus, the very thought of Thee
With sweetness fills my breast;
But sweeter far Thy face to see,
And in Thy presence rest.

No voice can sing, no heart can frame,
Nor can the memory find,
A sweeter sound than Thy blest name,
O Saviour of mankind!

O Hope of every contrite heart!
O Joy of all the meek!
To those who ask how kind Thou art,
How good to those who seek!

But what to those who find? Ah, this
Nor tongue nor pen can show;
The love of Jesus, what it is,
None but His loved ones know.

Jesus, our only joy be Thou,
As Thou our prize wilt be;
In Thee be all our glory now,
And through eternity.

Eleventh Century Latin Hymn (translated by Edward Caswall)

"HAIL THOU, WHO MAN'S REDEEMER ART"

Hail, Thou Who man's Redeemer art,
Jesu, the joy of every heart;
Great Maker of the world's wide fame,
And purest love's delight and flame.

* * * *

Our guide, our way to heavenly rest,
Be Thou the aim of every breast;

Be Thou the soother of our tears,
Our sweet reward above the spheres.

Roman Breviary (translated by T. Potter)

CHRISTMAS

Jesus, the Ransomer of man,
Who, ere created light began,
Didst from the sovereign Father spring,
His power and glory equalling.
The Father's light and splendor Thou,
Their endless hope to Thee that bow;
Accept the prayers and praise today
That through the world Thy servants pay.

Roman Breviary (translated by J. Neale and T. Potter)

HYMN

O Christ, the glorious Crown
Of virgins that are pure;
Who dost a love and thirst for Thee
Within their minds procure;
Thou art the spouse of those
That chaste and humble be,
The hope, the life, the only help
Of such as trust in Thee.

All charity of those
Whose souls Thy love doth warm;
All simple pleasures of such minds
As think no kind of harm;
All sweets delight wherewith
The patient hearts abound,
Do blaze Thy name, and with Thy praise
They make the world resound.

The sky, the land, the sea,
And all on earth below,

The glory of Thy worthy Name
Do with all their praises show.
The winter yields Thee praise,
And summer doth the same,
The sun, the moon, the stars and all
Do magnify Thy name.

The roses that appear
So fair in outward sight;
The violets which with their scent
Do yield so great delight;
The pearls, the precious stones,
The birds, Thy praise do sing,
The woods, the wells, and all delights,
Which from this earth do spring.

What creatures, O sweet Lord,
From praising Thee can stay?
What earthly thing but, filled with joy,
Thine honor doth betray?
Let us, therefore, with praise
Thy mighty works express,
With heart and hand, with mind, and all
Which we from Thee possess.

Blessed Philip Howard

FAIREST LORD JESUS

Fairest Lord Jesus
Ruler of all nature
O thou of God and man the Son!
Thee will I cherish,
Thee will I honor,
Thou my soul's glory, joy and crown.

Fair are the meadows,
Fairer still the woodlands,
Robed in the blooming garb of spring;

Jesus is fairer,
Jesus is purer,
Who makes the woeful heart to sing.

Fair is the sunshine,
Fairer still the moonlight,
And all the twinkling, starry host;
Jesus shines fairer
Jesus shines purer,
Than all the angels heaven can boast.

Anonymous (translated by R. Storrs Willis)

AT HIGH MASS

Thou who hast made this world so wondrous fair,—
The pomp of clouds; the glory of the sea;
Music of waters; song-birds' melody;
The organ of Thy thunder in the air;
Breath of the rose; and beauty everywhere—
Lord, take this stately service done to Thee,
The grave enactment of Thy Calvary
In jewelled pomp and splendor pictured there!

Lord, take the sounds and sights; the silk and gold;
The white and scarlet; take the reverent grace
Of ordered step; window and glowing wall—
Prophet and Prelate, holy men of old;
And teach us, children of the Holy Place
Who love Thy Courts, to love Thee best of all.

Robert Hugh Benson

"O LORD . . . HOW ADMIRABLE IS THY NAME"

O Lord our Lord, how admirable is thy name in the whole earth!
For thy magnificence is elevated above the heavens.
Out of the mouths of infants and of sucklings thou hast perfected praise, because of thy enemies, that thou mayst destroy the enemy and the avenger.

For I will behold thy heavens, the work of thy fingers: the moon and the stars which thou hast founded.
What is man that thou art mindful of him? or the son of man that thou visitest him?
Thou hast made him a little less than the angels, thou hast crowned him with glory and honor: and hast set him over the works of thy hands.

Psalm 8:2–7

From THE HOLY NAME OF JESUS

Welcome, dear, all-adored Name!
For sure there is no knee
That knows not Thee;
Or, if there be such sons of shame,
Alas! what will they do
When stubborn rocks shall bow,
And hills hang down their heaven-saluting heads,
To seek for humble beds
Of dust, where, in the bashful shades of night,
Next to their own low nothing they may lie,
And couch before the dazzling light of Thy dread Majesty?
They that by love's mild dictate now
Will not adore Thee
Shall then with just confusion bow
And break before Thee.

Richard Crashaw

WHIT SUNDAY

Fountain of Sweets! Eternal Dove!
Which leav'st Thy glorious perch above,
And hovering down, vouchsafest thus
To make Thy nest below with us.

Soft as Thy softest feathers, may
We find Thy love to us to-day;

And in the shelter of Thy wing
Obtain Thy leave and grace to sing.

Joseph Beaumont

A DOXOLOGY

Oh awful, mystic, Three-and-One—
The father, Holy Ghost, and Son!
Other in person and in name:
In life and nature, GOD, the same.

The Father first,—the only Son—
The Spirit, mingling Three-in-One;
All, gathered in their sole abode,
The very and eternal God.

There, when our day of peace began,
Throned in their midst, Behold the Man!
Jesu! the God who died, was he—
The Second of the awful Three.

Then fame and honor ever be,
In heaven, to GOD, the Trinity!
On earth, let equal praise be done,
And worship we the Three-and-One.

Robert Stephen Hawker

"SWEET STAR OF THE SEA!"

O purest of Creatures! sweet Mother! sweet Maid!
The one spotless womb wherein Jesus was laid!
Dark night hath come down on us, Mother! and we,
Look out for thy shining, sweet Star of the Sea!

Deep night hath come down on this rough-spoken world,
And the banners of darkness are boldly unfurl'd;
And the tempest-tost Church—all her eyes are on thee,
They look to thy shining, sweet Star of the Sea!

Anonymous, 19th Century (translated by Frederick W. Faber)

"VIRGIN, HAIL!"

Virgin, hail! alone the fairest!
Mother, who our Savior barest!
And the name of *Sea-Star* wearest,
  Star that leadest not astray!
On the sea of this life never
Let us suffer wreck, but ever
To Thy Savior, to deliver
  Those who travel o'er it, pray.

* * * *

Thou by Him wast pre-elected,
By Whom all things are directed,
Who thy maiden-mark protected,
  When thy sacred womb He filled;
Parent of our Savior-brother!
Thou didst feel nor pain nor other
Sorrow, like to man's first mother,
  When thou bringest forth that Child.

Mary! for thy merits wholly
Hast thou been uplifted solely,
O'er the choirs of angels holy,
  To a lofty throne above:
Joy is to this day pertaining,
When the heavens thou art gaining,
Then on us, below remaining,
  Look thou with maternal love!

Adam of St. Victor (translated by D. S. Wrangham)

TO THE BLESSED VIRGIN

'Twas not thy guileless faith alone
  That lifted thee so high;
'Twas not thy pure seraphic love,
  Or peerless chastity.
But O! it was thy lowliness,
  Well pleasing to the Lord

That made thee worthy to become
The Mother of the Word.

O loftiest! whose humility
So sweet it was to see!
That God, forgetful of Himself,
Abased Himself to thee.
Praise to the Father, with the Son
And Holy Ghost through whom
The Word Eternal was conceived
Within the Virgin's womb.

Anonymous (translated by Edward Caswall)

From *O GLORIOSA DOMINA*

Hail most high, most humble one!
Above the world; below thy Son,
Whose blush the moon beauteously mars
And stains the timorous light of stars.
He that made all things had not done
Till He had made Himself thy Son.
The whole world's Host would be thy Guest,
And board Himself at thy rich breast.
O boundless hospitality!
The Feast of all things feed on thee.

Richard Crashaw

LADY OF LORETTO

Hail holy Virgin Mary—Hail!
Whose tender mercies never fail;
Mother of Christ, of grace divine,
Of purity the spotless shrine,—
Mother of God, with virtues crown'd,
Most faithful—pitiful—renown'd
Deign from thy throne to look on me,
And hear my mournful Litany.

Madeline Bridges

GUARDIAN ANGEL

My oldest friend, mine from the hour
When first I drew my breath;
My faithful friend, that shall be mine,
Unfailing, till my death;

Thou hast ever been at my side:
My Maker to thy trust
Consigned my soul, what time He framed
The infant child of dust.

No beating heart in holy prayer,
No faith, informed aright,
Gave me to Joseph's tutelage,
Or Michael's conquering might.

Nor patron Saint, nor Mary's love,
The dearest and the best,
Has known my being, as thou hast known,
And blest, as thou hast blest.

Thou wast my sponsor at the font,
And thou, each budding year,
Didst whisper elements of truth
Into my childish ear.

And when, ere boyhood yet was gone,
My rebel spirit fell,
Ah! thou didst see, and shudder too,
Yet bear each deed of Hell.

And then in turn, when judgments came,
And scared me back again,
Thy quick soft breath was near to soothe
And hallow every pain.

Oh! who of all thy toils and cares
Can tell the tale complete,
To place me under Mary's smile,
And Peter's royal feet!

And thou wilt hang about my bed,
When life is ebbing low;
Of doubt, impatience, and of gloom,
The jealous sleepless foe.

Mine, when I stand before the Judge;
And mine, if spared to stay
Within the golden furnace, till
My sin is burned away.

And mine, O Brother of my soul,
When my release shall come;
Thy gentle arms shall lift me then,
Thy wings shall waft me home.

John Henry Newman

TO SAINT ANNE

Spotless Anna! Juda's glory!
Through the Church from east to west,
Every tongue proclaims thy praises,
Holy Mary's Mother blest!

Anonymous, 17th century (translated by Edward Caswall)

HYMN FOR HOLY INNOCENTS DAY

All hail! Ye Martyr Flowers,
Born with the blush of day,
Blossoms for Eden's bowers,
To grace Lord Jesu's way!

Young firstlings for the shrine,
Lambs of a tender fold,
Around the altars shine,
And palmy garlands hold.

Thee, Jesu! let us laud,
Child of a mother's love.

With Him the Father, God,
And that Eternal Dove.

Robert Stephen Hawker

FLOSCULUS IMMORTALIS

(A Christmas Prayer)

With the exception of the inimitable jasmine, which it is impossible to counterfeit, all flowers are perfectly represented by the blend of aromatic spirits. Joris Huysmans

O Jasmine of immortal years,
With sweetness which no art
Of man may simulate; send down
Your dew of fragrance on my heart
So long embattled with its horrent fears.
Rain down as soft as dew upon the grass.
"Rorate coeli desuper!" They pass,
These other flowers; the magic glass
Of one bright year beholds them fade
Narcissus-like into the shade
Of ashy nothingness. Dismayed
Am I, O Jasmine!
Young Immortal Jasmine, rain
Your arrowed scent upon me,
Tender pain!
O Vine
More bland than wine,
Bend down with sworded savors,
Hear my call!
What hands are these, what feet
To scale the wall
Which past the laughter of remotest star
Towers like music, where your flowers are?
Sweeter than hyacinthus, pink, or nard,
The rainbowed iris, or the lily white,
Fairer than lilacs, heaven-like thick-starred,
And moon flower in the quiet of the night.

O emblematic scent
Glad with all wonderment!
Eternal Jasmine, young as rose-bloom red
That burgeons when the dawn sings overhead,
Oh, set me free
From potent smell of every earthly bloom!
Flowers of the summer grass
They die, alas!
And You alone are sweet immortally.

Francis Beauchesne Thornton

LOVE: GOD'S LOVE FOR MAN, MAN'S LOVE OF GOD

"I WILL LOVE THEE, O LORD"

I will love thee, O Lord, my strength:
The Lord is my firmament, my refuge, and my deliverer.
My God *is* my helper, and in him will I put my trust.
My protector and the horn of my salvation, and my support.
Praising I will call upon the Lord: and I shall be saved from my
enemies. . . .
For thou lightest my lamp, O Lord: O my God enlighten my darkness.
For by thee I shall be delivered from temptation; and through my God
I shall go over a wall.
As for my God, his way is undefiled: the words of the Lord are fire tried:
he is the protector of all that trust in him.

Psalm 17:2–4, 29–31.

SUGGESTED BY ST. AUGUSTINE

What love I when I love Thee, O my God?
  Not corporal beauty, nor the limb of snow,
  Nor of loved light the white and pleasant flow,
Nor manna showers, nor streams that flow abroad,
Nor flowers of Heaven, nor small stars of the sod:
  Not these, my God, I love, who love Thee so;
  Yet love I something better than I know;—
A certain light on a more golden road;
A sweetness, not of honey or the hive;
  A beauty, not of summer or the spring;
  A scent, a music, and a blossoming
Eternal, timeless, placeless, without gyve,
  Fair, fadeless, undiminish'd, ever dim,—
  This, this is what I love in loving Him.

William Alexander

THE GOAL

Of all the prizes
That earth can give,
  This is the best:
To find Thee, Lord,
A living Presence near
  And in Thee rest!

Friends, fortune, fame,
Or what might come to me—
  I count all loss
If I find not
Companionship
  With Thee!

Anonymous

MY SPIRIT LONGETH FOR THEE

My spirit longeth for Thee,
  Within my troubled breast

Altho' I be unworthy
    Of so divine a Guest.

Of so divine a Guest,
    Unworthy tho' I be,
Yet has my heart no rest,
    Unless it come from Thee.

Unless it come from Thee,
    In vain I look around;
In all that I can see,
    No rest is to be found.

No rest is to be found,
    But in Thy blessèd love;
O! let my wish be crown'd,
    And send it from above!

John Byrom

BITTER-SWEET

Ah, my dear angry Lord,
Since Thou dost love, yet strike;
Cast down, yet help afford;
Sure I will do the like.

I will complain, yet praise,
I will bewail, approve;
And all my sour sweet days
I will lament, and love.

George Herbert

TO GOD THE FATHER

Great God: within whose simple essence, we
    Nothing but that which is Thy Self can find;
    When on Thyself Thou didst reflect, Thy mind

Thy thought was God, which took the form of Thee;
And when this God, thus born, Thou lov'st, and He
Loved Thee again, with passion of like kind,
As lovers' sighs which meet become one mind,
Both breathed one Spirit of equal deity.
Eternal Father, whence these two do come
And wil'st the title of my father have,
An heavenly knowledge in my mind engrave,
That it Thy Son's true Image may become:
Incense my heart with sighs of holy Love,
That it the temple of the Spirit may prove.

Henry Constable

"OH, WHEN A SOUL IS HID IN THEE"

Oh, when a soul is hid in Thee,
For what adventure can it yearn
Save love and still more love to learn,
And thus to love increasingly,
So deep does love within it burn?
My God, I pray Thee for a love
That yearns until I see Thy face,
And builds itself a nest above
Within its true abiding-place.

St. Teresa of Avila (translated by Allison Peers)

AMOR MYSTICUS

Let them say to my Lover
That here I lie!
The thing of His pleasure,
His slave am I.

Say that I seek Him
Only for love,
And welcome are tortures
My passion to prove.

Love giving gifts
Is suspicious and cold;
I have all, my Belovèd
When Thee I hold.

Hope and devotion
The good may gain;
I am but worthy
Of passion and pain.

So noble a Lord
None serves in vain,
For the pay of my love
Is my Love's sweet pain.

I love Thee, to love Thee,—
No more I desire;
By faith is nourished
My love's strong fire.

I kiss Thy hands
When I feel their blows;
In the place of caresses
Thou givest me woes.

But in Thy chastising
Is joy and peace.
O Master and Love,
Let Thy blows not cease.

Thy beauty, Belovèd,
With scorn is rife,
But I know that Thou lovest me
Better than life.

And because Thou invest me
Lover of mine,
Death can but make me
Utterly Thine.

I die with longing
Thy face to see;
Oh! sweet is the anguish
Of death to me!

Sister Marcela De Carpio (translated by John Hay)

GOD OUR REFUGE

If there had anywhere appeared in space
Another place of refuge where to flee,
Our hearts had taken refuge in that place,
And not with Thee.

For we against creation's bars had beat
Like prisoned eagles, through great worlds had sought
Though but a foot of ground to plant our feet,
Where Thou wert not.

And only when we found in earth and air,
In heaven or hell, that such might nowhere be—
That we could not flee from Thee anywhere,
We fled to Thee.

Richard C. Trench

THE MIRROR

Lord, make my soul
To mirror Thee,
Thyself alone
To shine in me,
That men may see
Thy love, Thy grace,
Nor note the glass
That shows Thy Face.

Blanche Mary Kelly

"I ASKED FOR PEACE"

I asked for Peace—
  My sins arose,
  And bound me close,
I could not find release.

I asked for Truth—
  My doubts came in,
  And with their din
They wearied all my youth.

I asked for Love—
  My lovers failed,
  And griefs assailed
Around, beneath, above.

I asked for Thee—
  And Thou didst come
  To take me home
Within Thy Heart to be.

Digby Mackworth Dolben

A SONG OF DIVINE LOVE

Lord, when the sense of thy sweet grace
Sends up my soul to seek thy face,
Thy blessèd eyes breed such desire
I die in love's delicious fire.
O love, I am thy sacrifice,
Be still triumphant, blessèd eyes.
Still shine on me, fair suns, that I
Still may behold though still I die.

Though still I die, I live again,
Still longing so to be still slain;
So gainful is such loss of breath,
I die even in desire of death.
Still live in me this loving strife

Of living death and dying life:
For while thou sweetly slayest me,
Dead to myself, I live in Thee.

Richard Crashaw

THE ASPIRATION

How long, Great God, how long must I
Immur'd in this dark prison lie;
Where at the grates and avenues of sense,
My soul must watch to have intelligence;
Where but faint gleams of Thee salute my sight,
Like doubtful moonshine in a cloudy night:
When shall I leave this magic sphere,
And be all mind, all eye, all ear?

How cold this clime! And yet my sense
Perceives e'en here Thy influence.
E'en here Thy strong magnetic charms I feel,
And pant and tremble like the amorous steel,
To lower good, and beauties less divine,
Sometimes my erroneous needle does decline,
But yet, so strong the sympathy,
It turns, and points again to Thee.

I long to see this excellence
Which at such distance strikes my sense.
My impatient soul struggles to disengage
Her wings from the confinement of her cage.
Wouldst thou, great Love, this prisoner once set free,
How would she hasten to be link'd to Thee!
She'd for no angels' conduct stay,
But fly, and love-on, all the way.

John Norris

ALL IN ALL

We know Thee, each in part—
A portion small;

But love Thee, as Thou art—
  The All in All:
For Reason and the rays thereof
Are starlight to the noon of Love.

John Banister Tabb

AS ONE FINDING PEACE

The secret of the King possesses me
Unutterably.
I am a child to sudden woman grown
Who never yet has known
Invasion so imperious, so complete,
Blindly and madly sweet.
I am a bud to sudden blossom blown,
Intoxicate, replete
With fragrance most divinely not its own.
I am dew thirstily drunk up
Out of dawn's lifted cup.
I am my own impotent, daring self, plunged in a sea
Ecstatically!

O God, encompass me!
Be infinitely mine to hold, to bound me;
Absorb, consume, encompass and confound me;
Be in me and beneath me and above me;
O Father, love me, love me!
Tremendously be,
Strong God, my sea.

In ultimate joy upon this Lover's breast
I come to rest.
Peace, like a song,
Envelopes me;
Peace, like the night,
Folds me in conscious, beautiful delight.
Never has human love held me in tranquil thrall,
For not to human love does peace belong.
What if I be for the Lord a wall,

Beauteous as cedar and as cedar strong;
What if I be a door, and sealed to all save Him,
Cunningly joined, guarded by flashing cherubim?
I am a door, a wall, tower of passionate strength
Around which multitudinously throng
Wild ecstasies, wild joys, unending blisses,
A God's caresses and a Father's kisses.

Presently let this rapture in profounder rapture cease;
A silver bulwark of wrought silence be,
My Father, since that I am come at length,
Captive and free,
Into Your presence as one finding peace.

Sister M. Madeleva

"O FLAME OF LIVING LOVE"

O flame of living love,
That dost eternally
Pierce through my soul with so consuming heat,
Since there's no help above,
Make thou an end of me,
And break the bond of this encounter sweet.

O burn that burns to heal!
O more than pleasant wound!
And O soft hand, O touch most delicate,
That dost new life reveal,
That dost in grace abound,
And, slaying, dost from death to life translate.

O lamps of fire that shined
With so intense a light,
That those deep caverns where the senses live,
Which were obsure and blind,
Now with strange glories bright,
Both heat and light to his beloved give.

With how benign intent
Rememberest thou my breast,
Where thou alone abidest secretly,
And in thy sweet ascent,
With glory and good possessed,
How delicately thou teachest love to me!

St. John of the Cross (translated by Arthur Symon)

ST. AUGUSTINE'S PRAYER

Imprint, O Lord! Thy wounds upon my heart,
That I, therein, Thy grief and love may see,
Grief, to endure for Thee all other griefs,
Love, to renounce all other Loves for Thee.

Translated by Eleanor C. Donnelly

LORD, IF THOU ART NOT PRESENT

Lord, if Thou art not present, where shall I
Seek Thee absent? If Thou art everywhere,
How is it that I do not see Thee nigh?

Thou dwellest in a light remote and fair,
How can I reach that light, Lord? I beseech
Thee, teach my seeking, and Thyself declare

Thyself, the sought to me. Unless Thou teach
Me, Lord, I cannot seek; nor can I find
Thee, if Thou wilt not come within my reach.

Lord, let me seek, with sturdy heart and mind,
In passion of desire and longingly.
Let me desire Thee, seeking Thee; and find—
Loving Thee, find Thee; love Thee, finding Thee.

John Gray

PETITION

My little lamp is almost empty, Lord;
The light is dim.
Fill it with sacrificial oil of pain,
Up to the brim.
Wash it with tears 'til crystal clear it shines;
Trim the wick right:
Then touch it with Thy love and it will give
Beautiful light.

Ruth Mary Fox

PRAYER OF ST. FRANCIS XAVIER

Thou art my God, sole object of my love;
Not for the hope of endless joys above;
Not for the fear of endless pains below,
Which they who love thee not must undergo.

For me, and such as me, thou deign'nst to bear
An ignominious cross, the nails, the spear;
A thorny crown transpierc'd thy sacred brow,
While bloody sweats from eve'ry member flow.

For me in tortures thou resign'd thy breath,
Embrac'd me on the cross, and sav'd me by thy death.
And can these sufferings fail my heart to move?
What but thyself can now deserve my love?

Such as then was, and is, thy love to me,
Such is, and shall be, still my love to thee—
To thee, Redeemer! mercy's sacred spring!
My God, my Father, Maker, and my King!

(Translated by Alexander Pope)

"IF LORD, THY LOVE FOR ME IS STRONG"

If Lord, Thy love for me is strong
As this which binds me unto Thee,

What holds me from Thee, Lord, so long,
What holds Thee, Lord, so long from me?

St. Teresa of Avila (translated by Arthur Symons)

GOD'S WAY

Dear Lord, You pleading asked a part
Of my already crowded heart:
And when with grudging, and with tears,
And thought of future lonely years,
I gave a part, ah, was it fair
To ask for a still larger share?

Ah, was it fair to ask a part,
And then with all a lover's art
To steal the whole? Ah, was it right
To use such sweet, tremendous might
Against a little, feeble soul
That feared the race, and feared the goal?

Florence Gilmore

"LORD, THOU THYSELF ART LOVE"

Lord, Thou Thyself art Love and only Thou;
Yet I who am not love would fain love Thee;
But Thou alone being Love canst furnish me
With that same love my heart is craving now.
Allow my plea! for if Thou disallow,
No second fountain can I find but Thee;
No second hope or help is left to me,
No second anything, but only Thou.
O Love, accept, according my request;
O Love, exhaust, fulfilling my desire:
Uphold me with the strength that cannot tire,
Nerve me to labor till Thou bid me rest,
Kindle my fire from Thine unkindled fire,
And charm the willing heart from out my breast.

Christina Rossetti

"I LIFT MY SOUL TO THEE"

But then, O God, I lift my soul to Thee:
As a hurt child flies to a mother's breast,
I fly to Thee with all my misery,
Pleading with piteous voice only for rest,
Rest from the world and all its vanity,
That in Thy love alone I may be blest.

John Lancaster Spalding

"O THOU, MY HEART'S DESIRE"

Eternal God! O Thou that only art
The sacred fountain of eternal light,
And blessed lodestone of my better part,
O Thou, my heart's desire, my soul's delight!
Reflect upon my soul, and touch my heart,
And then my heart shall prize no good above Thee;
And then my soul shall know Thee; knowing, love Thee;
And then my trembling thoughts shall never start
From Thy commands, or swerve the least degree,
Or once presume to move, but as they move in Thee.

Francis Quarles

BENEDICTION

Lord, dismiss us with Thy blessing,
Hope and comfort from above;
Let us each, Thy peace possessing,
Triumph in redeeming love.

Robert Stephen Hawker

LOVE TO DESTROY HATE

Lord,
Fill me with Thy love,
For I have got to meet

Hate in the world,
And I know well
That like will breed with like.
I would not add
Hate to hate,
But would attack
The very roots of hate
With alchemy
Of Love's providing,
So give to the roots
Of that most evil tree
No soil for sustenance.
Lord,
Fill me with Thy love
That so, at any cost,
Even in the midst of hate,
Love may go forth from me
In sacrifice
Like Thine.

Father Andrew

"I NEED THEE"

I need Thee, precious Jesus,
  I need a friend like Thee;
A friend to soothe and sympathize,
  A friend to care for me.

I need Thy heart, sweet Jesus,
  To feel each anxious care;
I long to tell my every want,
  And all my sorrows share.

* * * *

I'll need Thee, sweetest Jesus,
  When death's dread hour draws nigh,
To hide me in Thy sacred heart,
  Till wafted safe on high.

Anonymous

CORPUS CHRISTI

Jesus! my Lord, my God, my All!
How can I love Thee as I ought?
And how revere this wondrous gift,
So far surpassing hope or thought?

* * * *

Had I but Mary's sinless heart
To love Thee with, my dearest King!
O with what bursts of fervent praise
Thy goodness, Jesus, would I sing!
Sweet Sacrament! we Thee adore!
O make us love Thee more and more!

Frederick W. Faber

THE DEAR BARGAIN

Lord, what is man? why should he cost thee
So dear? what had his ruin lost thee?
Lord, what is man? that thou hast overbought
So much a thing of naught?

* * * *

What if my faithless soul and I
Would needs fall in
With guilt and sin,
What did the lamb, that he should die?
What did the lamb, that he should need,
When the wolf sins, himself to bleed?

If my base lust,
Bargain'd with death and well-beseeming dust
Why would the white
Lamb's bosom write
The purple name
Of my sin's shame?

Why should his unstain'd breast make good
My blushes with his own heart-blood?

O my Saviour, make me see
How dearly bought thou has paid for me

That lost again my life may prove
As then in death, so now in love.

Richard Crashaw

"O DO THOU NOT DEPART"

I think of Thee, O Christ, and I am strong;—
Again the way which Thou with blood did stain,
The narrow path of duty I regain,
And know God lives with him who does no wrong.
O keep me close to Thee, forever near
To Thy infinite loving, pitying heart:
In the lone night let me Thy voice still hear,
Or else I fall and suffer bruise and smart:
Thou only canst the dim-lit way make clear.
The hour is late: O do Thou not depart.

John Lancaster Spalding

CONTENTMENT

All the sweetness of Thee, Christ, I love.
Thou knowest—'tis no need to say what things—
And all the sweetness of Thine, Christ, I love,
Thine and mine too, because that we are one.
I hold my hands out wide, my fingers feel
The cool, the bright, the lovely drops of life
That come, and go, and stay not; that my tears
Once mingled with, because I could not keep
What I had looked upon and loved, much loved.
But life is Thine, and now no more I weep.
Thou lovest all. Thou lookest from above,
Standest beneath to catch, holdest with me
The running stream, while yet it runs from me.
Thou lovest all. It is enough. Amen.

Jacqueline Noble

MAY THE SWEET NAME OF JESUS

May the sweet name of Jesus
Be lovingly graven
In my heart's inmost haven.

O Mary, Blest Mother,
Be Jesus my Brother,
And I Jesu's lover.

A binding of love
That no distance can sever,
Be between us for ever,
    Yea, O my Saviour,
    For ever and ever.

Anonymous (translated from the Gaelic by Eleanor Hull)

EASTER

Most glorious Lord of life, that on this day,
    didst make thy triumph over death and sin:
and having harrowed hell, didst bring away
captivity thence captive us to win:
This joyous day, dear Lord, with joy begin,
    and grant that we for whom thou diddest die
    being with thy dear blood clean washed from sin,
may live for ever in felicity.
And that thy love we weighing worthily,
    may likewise love thee for the same again:
    and for thy sake that all like dear didst buy,
    with love may one another entertain.
So let us love, dear love, like as we ought,
    love is the lesson which the Lord us taught.

Edmund Spenser

ASCENSION HYMN

O Christ, who mountest up the sky
To deck fair thrones for us on high,

Thine exiled sons in love restore
Unto their native land once more.

There gifts to all Thou dost afford,
Thyself shall be our great reward;
How brief below our time of pain!
How long our pleasure shall remain!

With eye unveiled and sated heart
We there shall see Thee as Thou art,
And tell in hymns of sweet accord
Our love and praise of Thee, O Lord.

Lest we be orphaned of Thy love,
Send down from Thy high halls above
The Spirit of adoption sweet,
Salvation's pledge, the Paraclete.

Jesu, to Thee our anthems tend,
We shall be judged at time's last end;
To God the Father equal praise
And Holy Ghost through endless days.

Jean Baptiste de Santeul (translated by Allan G. McDougall)

TO OUR BLESSED LADY

Mother of mercy! day by day
My love of thee grows more and more;
Thy gifts are strewn upon my way,
Like sands upon the great sea-shore.

* * * *

Jesus, when His three hours were run,
Bequeath'd thee from the Cross to me,
And oh! how can I love thy Son,
Sweet Mother! if I love not thee.

Frederick W. Faber

SUBMISSION TO GOD

"THE LORD RULETH ME"

The Lord ruleth me, and I shall want nothing. He hath set me in a place of pasture.
He hath brought me up, on the water of refreshment: he hath converted my soul.
He hath led me on the path of justice, for his own name's sake.
For though I should walk in the midst of the shadow of death,
I will fear no evils, for thou art with me.

Psalm 22:1–4

PRAYER AGAINST ALIEN REST

Let not, O God, the feet of my exploring mind,
Skimming the wasteful waters of the dark,
The firmness of far resting-places find;
But, like the dove returning to the ark,
Bear potent proof there is no surer rest
Than here, exploring ended, with a Guest,
Whose nearness is as wings none see,
All hear, stirring the night of mystery.

Sister Miriam

AN OFFERING

Only a broken vessel, Lord,
I offer Thee to-day,
A lowly, broken vessel, Lord,
Made out of sinful clay.

'T was fashioned once of fairest form,
A goodly, holy sight,
When Thy kind hand had moulded it,
And blessed it with Thy light.

'T was meant to be for Thee alone,
Thy gift alone to hold;
Oh, it was shining, dazzling bright,
Like lustrous beaten gold.

Ah, had I ever kept it so,
A treasure for Thy grace,
It would not be so worthless now
Before Thy holy face.

And I with earth's delusive gifts
Did fill this vessel fair;
Alas, they were a foulsome weight
The vessel could not bear.

Behold, O Lord, how many a scar,
How many a deadly seam;
Where once was all so glorious,
Where Heavenly light did gleam.

I shudder, Lord,—wilt Thou accept
Such lowly gift as this?
Unlovely vessel fouled by sin,
Yet yearning now for bliss.

Ah, Lord, I needs must cry despair,
Didst Thou not speak to me;
A broken heart, repaired in grief,
Will be received by Thee?

So, Lord, this broken vase is Thine;
Come with Thy grace to fill;
And may it ever near Thy heart
Love's perfume sweet distill.

Hugh Francis Blunt

SUBMISSION

Since to my smiting enemy
Thou biddest me be meek,
Lo, gladlier, my God, to Thee
I turn the other cheek.

John Banister Tabb

"LORD OF THE WINDS"

Lord of the winds, I cry to Thee,
I that am dust,
And blown about by every gust
I fly to Thee.

Lord of the waters, unto Thee I call.
I that am weed upon the waters borne,
And by the waters torn,
Tossed by the waters, at Thy feet I fall.

Mary Coleridge

SURRENDER

The Lord bless us, and keep us,
and shew the light of His countenance upon us,
And be merciful unto us,
The Lord lift up His countenance upon us,
And give us peace!
I commend to Thee, O Lord,
my soul, and my body,
my mind, and my thoughts,
my prayers, and my vows,
my senses, and my limbs,
my words, and my works,
my life, and my death;
my brothers, and my sisters,
and their children;
my friends, my benefactors, my well wishers,
those who have a claim on me;
my kindred, and my neighbours,
my country, and all Christendom.
I commend to Thee, Lord,
my impulses, and my startings,
my intentions, and my attempts,
my going out, and my coming in,
my sitting down, and my rising up.

Lancelot Andrewes (translated by John Henry Newman)

THE RECOMMENDATION

These Hours, and that which hovers o'er my End,
Into Thy hands, and heart, Lord, I commend.

Take both to Thine account, that I and mine
In that Hour, and in these, may all be Thine.

That as I dedicate my devoutest Breath
To make a kind of Life for my Lord's Death,

So from His living, and life-giving Death,
My dying Life may draw a new, and never fleeting Breath.

Richard Crashaw

"O LOVE THAT WILL NOT LET ME GO"

O Love that will not let me go,
I rest my weary soul in Thee;
I give Thee back the life I owe,
That in Thine ocean depths its flow
May richer, fuller, be.

O Light that followest all my way,
I yield my flickering torch to Thee;
My heart restores its borrowed ray,
That in Thy sunshine's blaze its day
May brighter, fairer, be.

O Joy that seekest me through pain,
I cannot close my heart to Thee;
I trace the rainbow through the rain,
And feel the promise is not vain
That morn shall tearless be.

O Cross that liftest up my head,
I dare not ask to fly from Thee;
I lay in dust life's glory dead,
And from the ground there blossoms red
Life that shall endless be.

George Matheson

A HYMN TO CHRIST, AT THE AUTHOR'S LAST GOING INTO GERMANY

In what torn ship soever I embark,
That ship shall be my emblem of thy ark;
What sea soever swallow me, that flood
Shall be to me an emblem of thy blood;
Though thou with clouds of anger to disguise
Thy face: yet through that mask I know those eyes,
  Which though they turn away sometimes,
    They never will despise.

I sacrifice this island unto thee,
And all whom I love'd there, and who lov'd me;
When I have put our seas twixt them and me,
Put thou thy sea betwixt my sins and thee.
As the trees' sap doth seek the root below
In winter, in my winter now I go,
  Where none but thee, th' eternal root
    Of true Love I may know.

* * * *

Seal then this bill of my divorce to all,
On whom those fainter beams of love did fall;
Marry those loves, which in youth scattered be
On Fame, Wit, Hopes (false mistresses) to thee.
Churches are best for prayer, that have least light:
To see God only, I go out of sight:
  And to 'scape stormy days, I choose
    An everlasting night.

John Donne

NEW YEAR'S GIFT

'Tis custom, Lord, this day to send
A gift to every common friend;
And shall I find no gift for Thee,
That art the best of friends to me?
There's nothing which my thoughts survey—

My life, my soul, the light, the day—
But they are all Thy gifts to me.
And shall I find no gift for Thee?
Yea, Lord, behold I now confer
My life, my soul, and whatso'er
Thy liberal hand hath given me
Back as a New Year's gift to Thee.

Nathaniel Eaton

"GOD! THE ONE, THE ALL OF BEING!"

God! the one, the All of Being! let me lose my life in Thine;
Let me be what Thou hast made me, be a quiver of Thy flame.
Purge my self from self's pollution; burn it into life divine;
Burn it till it dies triumphant in the firespring when it came.

Edmond Gore Alexander Holmes

FAIN WOULD MY THOUGHTS

Fain would my thoughts fly up to Thee,
Thy peace, sweet LORD, to find;
But when I offer, still the world
Lays clogs upon my mind.

Sometimes I climb a little way
And thence look down below;
How nothing there, do all things seem,
That here make such a show!

Then round about I turn my eyes
To feast my hungry sight;
I meet with Heaven in every thing,
In every thing delight.

When I have thus triumph'd awhile,
And think to build my nest,
Some cross conceits come fluttering by,
And interrupt my rest.

Then to the earth again I fall,
And from my low dust cry,
'Twas not in my wing, LORD, but Thine,
That I got up so high.

And now, my God, whether I rise,
Or still lie down in dust,
Both I submit to Thy blest will;
In both, on Thee I trust.

Guide Thou my way, who art Thyself
My everlasting end,
That every step, or swift, or slow,
Still to Thyself may tend!

To Father, Son, and Holy Ghost,
One consubstantial Three,
All highest praise, all humblest thanks,
Now and for ever be!

John Austin

SINCE FIRST THY WORD

Since first Thy Word awaked my heart,
Like new life dawning o'er me,
Where'er I turn mine eyes, Thou art,
All light and love before me.
Nought else I feel, or hear or see—
All bonds of earth I sever—
Thee, O God, and only Thee
I live for, now and ever.

Like him whose fetters dropp'd away
When light shone o'er his prison,
My spirit, touch'd by Mercy's ray,
Hath from her chains arisen.
And shall a soul Thou bidst be free,
Return to bondage?—never!

Thee, O God, and only Thee
I live for, now and ever.

Thomas Moore

THY WILL BE DONE IN ME

O Thou to whom, without reserve,
My all I would resign,
I ask for grace and faith to say,
"Thy will, O Lord, not mine!"
In joy or grief, in bliss or pain,
This prayer shall rise to Thee,
"Thy will, not mine, O blessed Lord,
Thy will be done in me!"

Though thorns may pierce my weary feet,
Yet would I ne'er repine,
But meekly say, as Thou hast said,
"Thy will, O Lord, not mine!"
And though I pass beneath Thy rod,
Amen, so let it be!
Whate'er Thou wilt, O blessed Lord,
I know is best for me.

So would I live that I may feel
Thy perfect peace divine,
And still Thy pure example show
In every act of mine;
And till I reach the silent vale,
And cross the narrow sea,
Be this my prayer, O blessed Lord,
"Thy will be done in me!"

Fanny Crosby

"IN HAVING ALL THINGS"

In having all things, and not Thee, what have I?
Not having Thee what have my labors got?

Let me enjoy but Thee, what further crave I?
And having Thee alone, what have I not?
I wish nor sea nor land; nor would I be
Possess'd of heaven, heaven unpossess'd of Thee.

Francis Quarles

DEDICATION

Holy Jesus, Thou art born
For my sake on Christmas morn.
Lord, as Thou art born for me,
I am born again to Thee.

Through the city and abroad,
Thou dost lead me unto God,
Wheresoe'er Thou leadest me,
Master, I will follow Thee.

To Thy love my love I give,
Thou dost die that I may live.
As Thou giv'st Thy life for me,
Lord, I give my life to Thee.

From the tomb I see Thee rise,
When the morning fills the skies.
Lord, as Thou art risen for me,
I will rise from death to Thee.

Victoria Saffelle Johnson

"JESUS, I MY CROSS HAVE TAKEN"

Jesus, I my cross have taken,
All to leave and follow Thee;
I am poor, despised, forsaken,—
Thou henceforth my all shall be:
Perish every fond ambition,—
All I've sought, or hoped, or known;

Yet how rich is my condition,—
God and heaven may be mine own!

Madeline Bridges

DISCOVERY

O blessed God, O Savior sweet,
O Jesus, look on me!
O Christ, my King, refuse me not,
Though late I come to Thee!

I come to Thee, confounded quite
With sorrow and with shame,
When I beheld Thy bitter wounds
And knew I did the same.

Venerable Nicholas Postgate

"JESUS, ALL HAIL"

Jesus! all hail, Who for my sin
Didst die, and by that death didst win
Eternal life for me;
Send me Thy grace, good Lord! that I
Unto the world and flesh may die,
And hide my life with Thee.

Jesus! from out Thine open side
Thou hast the thirsty world supplied
With endless streams of love;
Come ye who would your sickness quell,
Draw freely from that sacred well,
Its heavenly virtues prove.

Anonymous (translated by Frederick W. Faber)

RESOLUTION

Love, You have struck me straight, my Lord!
Past innocence, past guilt,

I carry in my soul the sword
 You buried to the hilt.

And though to eyes in terrible pain
 Heaven and soul may reel,
For fear You may not strike again
 I will not draw the steel.

Charles L. O'Donnell

TO CHRIST CRUCIFIED

 O Saviour sweet, hear my request,
Make me partner of Thy pain;
In solace never let me rest,
Sith Thou in sorrow dost remain.

And if it be Thy glorious will,
That I shall taste of this Thy cup,
Lo, here Thy pleasure to fulfil,
Myself I wholly offer up.

Blessed Swithin Wells

ANIMA CHRISTI

Soul of Christ, be my sanctification;
Body of Christ, be my salvation;
Blood of Christ, fill all my veins;
Water of Christ's side, wash out my stains;
Passion of Christ, my comfort be;
O good Jesu, listen to me;
In Thy Wounds I fain would hide,
Ne'er to be parted from Thy side;
Guard me, should the foe assail me;
Call me when my life shall fail me;
Bid me come to Thee above,
With Thy saints to sing Thy love,
 World without end. Amen.

St. Ignatius Loyola (translated by John Henry Newman)

"O CHRIST, MY LORD"

O Christ, my Lord, which for my sins didst hang upon a tree,
Grant that Thy grace in me poor wretch may still ingrafted be.

Grant that Thy naked hanging there, may kill in me all pride
And care of wealth, since Thou didst then in such poor state abide.

Blessed Philip Howard

"MAKE OF MY SOUL"

Make of my soul, O Lord
  A cloak to wrap Thy body crucified.
Make of my mortal frame
  A temple for Thy dwelling place.
Make of my mind a lantern
  For the wisdom of Thy Faith.
Make of my hand a gauntlet
  To wield the shining sword of Truth.
Make of my heart a torch
  To light the way to Thee.

William Noé Field

THE LITTLE GIFT

O, with a gesture light and free,
Lord, I would give my life to Thee—
Not solemnly
Not grudgingly.

No! I would take my life and fling
It at Thy feet, and sing, and sing,
So I might bring
Thee this small thing!

Mary Dixon Thayer

BATTER MY HEART

Batter my heart, three-personed God; for you
As yet but knock; breath, shine, and seek to mend;
That I may rise and stand, o'erthrow me, and bend
Your force, to break, blow, burn, and make me new.
I, like an usurped town, to another due,
Labour to admit you, but oh, to no end;
Reason, your viceroy in me, me should defend,
But is captived, and proves weak or untrue.
Yet dearly I love you, and would be lovèd fain,
But am betrothed unto your enemy;
Divorce me, untie, or break that knot again,
Take me to you, imprison me, for I,
Except you enthrall me, never shall be free;
Nor ever chaste, except you ravish me.

John Donne

WITH FRANKINCENSE AND MYRRH

I bring no gifts in cellophane;
no tinsel rain,

no brave red ribbon, mistletoe;
no altar glow,

no tryptich and no Gobelin—
only my sin.

Others have brought you spruce and holly.
I bring my folly.

My greed, my pride, my hot conceit
lie at your feet.

They cost me all my meager hoard.
Receive them, Lord.

Jennie M. Palen

THE CUP

Sweet Lord, I fear
  This cup of dread—
These shames and fears,
  These toils and throes.
Oh, give a clear
  Cool draught instead;
I cannot drink this cup of woes!

Thou takest now
  The fearsome cup?—
  The holy lips to bless the brink!—
Nay, lest that thou
  Shouldst drink it up,
  Give me the draught—I drink! I drink!

Edward F. Garesché

SWIMMER'S PRAYER

Let me lean upon your will, O God!
As the swimmer leans upon the sinews of the water.
I do not ask to tread as Peter trod
Or move with fish-like majesty, unmindful
Of the air men breathe. Give
But the easy confidence of any supple
Swimmer in the water, and let me live
In You and move as men are meant to live and move.
And finally, my gasp-for-your-life breath,
Grasp-at-a-straw stroke, smooth
To the rhythm of him whom death
Strikes as a buoyancy and not a void.

Sister Mary Davida

FAITH: PLEDGES AND PLEAS

"IN THEE . . . I PUT MY TRUST"

To thee, O Lord, have I lifted up my soul. In thee, O my God, I put my trust; let me not be ashamed.
Neither let my enemies laugh at me: for none of them that wait on thee shall be confounded.
Let all them be confounded that act unjust things without cause.
Shew, O Lord, thy ways to me, and teach me thy paths.
Direct me in thy truth, and teach me; for thou art God my Saviour; and on thee have I waited all the day long.
Remember, O Lord, thy bowels of compassion; and thy mercies that are from the beginning of the world.
The sins of my youth and my ignorances do not remember.
According to thy mercy remember thou me: for thy goodness' sake, O Lord.

Psalm 24:1–7

"I AM THE WAY"

Thou art the Way.
Hadst Thou been nothing but the goal,
I cannot say
If Thou hadst ever met my soul.

I cannot see—
I, child of process—if there lies
An end for me,
Full of repose, full of replies.

I'll not reproach
The road that winds, my feet that err.
Access, Approach
Art Thou, Time, Way, and Wayfarer.

Alice Meynell

NO OTHER CHOICE

Doth Earth send nothing up to Thee but moans,
Father? Canst Thou find melody in groans?
O, can it be that Thou, the God of bliss,
Canst feed Thy glory on a world like this?

Yet it is well with us. From these alarms
Like children scared we fly into Thine arms;
And pressing sorrows put our pride to rout
With a swift faith which has not time to doubt.

We cannot herd in peace with wild beasts rude;
We dare not live in Nature's solitude;
In how few eyes of men can we behold
Enough of love to make us calm and bold?

O, it is well with us! With angry glance
Life glares at us, or looks at us askance:

Seek where will—Father, we see it now!—
None love us, trust us, welcome us, but Thou.

Frederick W. Faber

CANTICLE OF WEAKNESS

Then let my feet be stoutly shod in frailty;
For helmet, grant me only knowledge of thyself;
Give me to wear my weakness manfully—
Knowing it for armor
And for camouflage.

O God of Battles,
I have hungered for strength as for bread;
Yet I have held infirmity in honor
As a charger that has borne me well in the fray,
As a sword that is fitted for smiting.

For I have thirsted mightily for thy glory,
O Omnipotence,
And Thy stand is adamant:
"I have chosen the weak to confound the strong."

Look upon me, O King and Captain,
And see that I am weak enought to conquer,
Trusting in Thee.

Sister Mary Paulinus

FAITH AND CONTENT

My Lord, how full of sweet content,
I pass my years of banishment!
Where'er I dwell, I dwell with Thee,
In Heaven, in earth, or on the sea.

To me remains nor place nor time;
My country is in every clime;

I can be calm and free from care
On any shore, since God is there.

Madame Guyon (translated by William Cowper)

AFTER ST. AUGUSTINE

Sunshine let it be or frost,
   Storm or calm, as Thou shalt choose;
Though Thine every gift were lost,
   Thee Thyself we could not lose.

Mary Coleridge

THE WILL OF GOD

I worship Thee, sweet will of God!
And all Thy ways adore;
And every day I live, I long
To love thee more and more.

When obstacles and trials seem
Like prison-walls to be,
I do the little I can do,
And leave the rest to Thee.

Frederick W. Faber

ACT OF FAITH

Great God, whatever through Thy Church
   Thou teachest to be true,
   I firmly do believe it all,
   And will confess it too.
Thou never canst deceived be,
   Thou never canst deceive,
For Thou art Truth itself, and Thou
   Dost tell me to believe.

Anonymous

"O GIFTS OF GIFTS"

O gifts of gifts! O grace of faith!
My God! how can it be
That Thou, Who hast discerning love,
Shouldst give that gift to me?

Frederick W. Faber

CONVERSION

But gracious God, how well dost Thou provide
For erring judgments an unerring guide!
Thy throne is darkness in the abyss of light,
A blaze of glory that forbids the sight.
O teach me to believe Thee thus concealed,
And search no farther than Thy self revealed;
But her alone for my director take,
Whom Thou has promised never to forsake!
My thoughtless youth was winged with vain desires;
My manhood, long misled by wandering fires,
Followed false lights; and when their glimpse was gone,
My pride struck out new sparkles of her own.
Such was I, such by nature still I am;
Be Thine the glory and be mine the shame!

John Dryden

THE IMAGE OF GOD

O Lord! who seest from yon starry height,
Centered in one, the future and the past,
Fashioned in thine own image, see how fast
The world obscures in me what once was bright
Eternal Sun! the warmth which thou hast given
To cheer life's flowery April, fast decays;
Yet, in the hoary winter of my days,
Forever green shall be my trust in heaven.

Celestial King! oh, let thy presence pass
Before my spirit, and an image fair
Shall meet that look of mercy from on high,
As the reflected image in a glass
Doth meet the look on him who seeks it there,
And owes its being to the gazer's eye.

Francisco De Aldana (translated by H. W. Longfellow)

PRAYER BESIDE THE MANGER

There in the narrow manger bleak and cold
My Lord Thou art;
And there within those Hands, so soft and weak,
I lay my heart.
Beneath those tiny Feet I bow my head,
O blessed Child;
And kiss the straw that forms Thy chilly bed
In winter wild.

* * * *

Upon Thy fair and youthful face I read
A look of love—
A look which bids me trust Thee in my need,
Spouse of the Dove.
Mother of God, commend me to thy Son
As here I bend;
And, oh, commend me when my task is done,
And life shall end.

A sinner kneeling at an Infant's cot
I call on Thee;
A sinner at the Cross forget me not,
But plead for me.
And thus in faith assured I leave my heart,
Blest Child with Thee;
A worthless gift with which Thou wilt not part
Eternally.

Anonymous

HYMN

Let me not stray,
  Dear Saviour, lost and weary,
Out from the narrow way,
  The wide is still more dreary;
  But let one star,
    Shine fore'er o'er me,
  Though faint and far,
    Be still before me.

Help me to bear
  My faith in Thee unbroken;
Thou hearest prayer
  E'en though unspoken;
    Grant me above the cross
      The crown to see—
    Heaven nearer by each loss
      That falls on me!

Madeline Bridges

KNOWLEDGE THROUGH SUFFERING

I knew Thee not, Thou wounded Son of God,
Till I with Thee the path of suffering trod;
Till in the valley, through the gloom of night,
I walked with Thee, and turned to Thee for light.

I did not know the mystery of love,
The love that doth the fruitless branch remove;
The love that spares not e'en the fruitful tree,
But prunes, that it may yet more fruitful be.

I did not know the meaning of the Cross;
I counted it but bitterness and loss:
Till in Thy gracious discipline of pain
I found the loss I dreaded purest gain.

And shall I cry, e'en on the darkest day,
"Lord of all mercy, take my cross away"?
Nay, in the Cross I saw Thine open face,
And found therein the fulness of Thy grace.

George Wallace Briggs

"LORD, IT BELONGS NOT TO MY CARE"

Lord, it belongs not to my care,
  Whether I die or live;
To love and serve Thee is my share,
  And this Thy grace must give.

If life be long I will be glad,
  That I may long obey;
If short—yet why should I be sad
  To soar to endless day?

CHRIST leads me through no darker rooms
  Than He went through before;
He that unto GOD's kingdom comes,
  Must enter by this door.

Come, LORD, when grace has made me meet
  Thy blessèd face to see;
For if Thy work on earth be sweet,
  What will Thy glory be!

Then I shall end my sad complaints,
  And weary, sinful days;
And join with the triumphant saints,
  To sing JEHOVAH's praise.

My knowledge of that life is small,
  The eye of faith is dim;
But 'tis enough that CHRIST knows all,
  And I shall be with Him.

Richard Baxter

"O JESUS CHRIST, REMEMBER"

O Jesus Christ, remember,
  When Thou shalt come again,
Upon the clouds of heaven,
  With all Thy shining train;—
When every eye shall see Thee
  In Deity reveal'd,
Who now upon this altar
  In silence art concealed.

* * * *

Remember then, O Savior,
  I supplicate of Thee,
That here I bow'd before Thee
  Upon my bended knee;
That here I own'd Thy presence,
  And did not Thee deny;
And glorified Thy greatness
  Though hid from human eye.

Edward Caswall

FAITH FOR ALL

We feel and see with different hearts and eyes:—
  Ah Christ, if all our hearts could meet in Thee,
  How well it were for them and well for me,
Our hearts Thy dear accepted sacrifice.
Thou, only Life of hearts and Light of eyes,
  Our life, our light, if once we turn to Thee,
  So be it, O Lord, to them and so to me;
Be all alike Thine own dear sacrifice.
Thou Who by death hast ransomed us from death,
  Thyself God's sole well-pleasing Sacrifice,
    Thine only sacred Self I plead with Thee:
    Make Thou it well for them and well for me
That Thou hast given us souls and wills and breath,
  And hearts to love Thee, and to see Thine eyes.

Christina Rossetti

AN ACT OF HOPE

My God, I firmly hope in Thee,
For Thou art great and good;
Thou gavest us Thine only Son
To die upon the Rood.
I hope through Him for grace to live
As Thy commandments teach,
And through Thy mercy, when I die
The joys of heaven to reach.

Anonymous

CONFIDENCE

Thou layest Thy hand on the fluttering heart
And sayest, "Be still!"
The shadow and silence are only a part
Of Thy sweet will.
Thy Presence is with me, and where Thou art
I fear no ill.

Frances Ridley Havergal

From O WHITHER SHALL I FLY

Great God! there is no safety here below;
Thou art my fortress, thou that seem'st my foe.
'Tis thou, that strik'st the stroke, must guard the blow.

Thou art my God, by thee I fall or stand;
Thy grace hath given me courage to withstand
All tortures, but my conscience and thy hand.

I know thy justice is thyself; I know,
Just God, thy very self is mercy too;
If not to thee, where, whither shall I go?

Then work thy will; if passion bid me flee,
My reason shall obey; my wings shall be
Stretch'd out no further than from thee to thee.

Francis Quarles

PRAYER AND FAITH

Lord, what a change within us one short hour
Spent in thy presence will avail to make—
What heavy burdens from our bosoms take,
What parchéd grounds refresh as with a shower!
We kneel, and all around us seems to lower;
We rise, and all, the distant and the near,
Stands forth in sunny outline, brave and clear;
We kneel, how weak; we rise, how full of power!
Why, therefore, should we do ourselves this wrong,
Or others—that we are not always strong;
That we are overborne with care,
That we should ever weak or heartless be,
Anxious or troubled, when with us is prayer,
And joy and strength and courage are with thee?

Richard C. Trench

"DEAR LORD, THOU KNOWEST WHEN I PRAY"

Dear Lord, Thou knowest when I pray
I have not many words to say;
I do but kneel, and offer Thee
All that I am, all I might be.

Do others render Thee more praise
With eloquent gesture and phrase?
I only dare to clasp Thy feet,
I only know that Thou art sweet.

Teach me, dear Lord, Thyself to find
In every lovely thing;

Teach Thou mine eyes, for they are blind;
Teach Thou my heart to sing!

I cannot ever know Thee, Lord,
Unless Thou aidest me,
I grope in darkness for Thy hand—
"Lord, Lord, that I may see!"

Stoop down and whisper in my heart,
"Fear not, for I am near."
But when Thou speakest—then, O then
Enable me to hear!

Mary Dixon Thayer

FOR GRACE

"GIVE ME UNDERSTANDING"

Set before me for a law the way of thy justifications, O Lord: and I will always seek after it.

Give me understanding, and I will search thy law; and I will keep it with my whole heart.

Lead me into the path of thy commandments; for this samc I have desired.

Incline my heart into thy testimonies and not to covetousness.

Turn away my eyes that they may not behold vanity: quicken me in thy way. . . .

Let thy mercy also come upon me, O Lord: thy salvation according to thy word.

So shall I answer them that reproach me in any thing; that I have trusted in thy words.

And take thou not the word of truth utterly out of my mouth: for in thy words, I have hoped exceedingly.

So shall I always keep thy law, for ever and ever.

Psalm 118: 33–37, 41–44.

A PARAPHRASE ON THOMAS À KEMPIS
(Done by Alexander Pope when he was Age Twelve)

Speak, gracious Lord, oh speak; Thy servant hears:
For I'm Thy servant and I'll still be so:
Speak words of comfort in my willing ears;
And since my tongue is in Thy praises slow,
And since that Thine all rhetoric exceeds,
Speak Thou in words, but let me speak in deeds!

Nor speak alone, but give me grace to hear
What Thy celestial sweetness does impart;
Let it not stop when entered at the ear,
But sink, and take deep rooting in my heart.
As the parched earth drinks rain (but grace afford)
With such a gust will I receive Thy word.

Nor with the Israelites shall I desire
Thy heavenly word by Moses to receive,
Lest I should die; but Thou who didst inspire
Moses himself, speak Thou, that I may live.
Rather with Samuel I beseech with tears,
Speak, gracious Lord, oh speak; Thy servant hears.

* * * *

Let them be silent then; and Thou alone,
My God! speak comfort to my ravish'd ears;
Light of my eyes, my Consolation,
Speak when Thou wilt, for still Thy Servant hears.
Whate'er Thou speak'st, let this be understood:
Thy greater Glory, and my greater Good!

Alexander Pope

"MY GOD, I HEARD THIS DAY"

My God, I heard this day
That none doth build a stately habitation
But he that means to dwell therein.
What house more stately hath there been,

Or can be, then is Man? to whose creation
All things are in decay.

* * * *

Since then, my God, Thou hast
So brave a place built, O dwell in it,
That it may dwell with Thee at last!
Till then afford us so much wit,
That, as the world serves us, we may serve Thee,
And both Thy servants be.

George Herbert

A PRAYER FOR AID

Oh, make me see Thee, Lord, where'er I go!
If mortal beauty sets my soul on fire,
That flame when near to Thine must needs expire,
And I with love of only Thee shall glow.
Dear Lord, Thy help I seek against this woe,
These torments that my spirit vex and tire;
Thou only with new strength canst re-inspire
My will, my sense, my courage faint and low.
Thou gavest me on earth this soul divine;
And Thou within this body weak and frail
Didst prison it—how sadly there to live!
How can I make its lot less vile than mine?
Without Thee, Lord, all goodness seems to fail.
To alter fate is God's prerogative.

Michelangelo (translated by John Addington Symonds)

FOR INSPIRATION

The prayers I make will then be sweet indeed,
If thou the spirit give by which I pray;
My unassisted heart is barren clay,
Which of its native self can nothing feed;

Of good and pious works thou art the seed
  Which quickens where thou say'st it may;
  Unless thou show us then thine own true way,
No man can find it! Father, Thou must lead!
Do thou, then, breathe those thoughts into my mind
  By which such virtue may in me be bred
  That in thy holy footsteps I may tread:
The fetters of my tongue do thou unbind,
  That I may have the power to sing of thee
  And sound thy praises everlastingly.

Michelangelo (translated by William Wordsworth)

ANGUISH

My God and King! to Thee
  I bow my knee;
I bow my troubled soul, and greet
With my foul heart thy holy feet.
Cast it, or tread it! it shall do
Even what thou wilt, and praise thee too.

My God, could I weep blood,
  Gladly I would,
Or if thou wilt give me that art,
Which through the eyes pours out the heart,
I will exhaust it all, and make
Myself all tears, a weeping lake.

O! 'tis an easy thing
  To write and sing;
But to write true, unfeigned verse
Is very hard! O God, disperse
These weights, and give my spirit leave
To act as well as to conceive!

O my God, hear my cry;
  Or let me die!

Henry Vaughan

TO THE BLESSED VIRGIN

Do not despise, O most glorious one,
The prayers of those who faithfully beseech thee,
But receive them and present them
To your Son God, O immaculate one,
To Him Who is our only Benefactor,
While we have you as our patron.

Attributed to St. John Damascus

RESURGAM

Teach me, O God, to bear my cross,
As Thine was borne;
Teach me to make every loss
A crown of thorns.
Give me Thy patience and Thy strength
With every breath,
Until my lingering days at length
Shall welcome death.

Dear Jesus, I believe that Thou
Didst rise again,
Instill the spirit in me now
That conquers pain.
Give me the grace to cast aside
All vain desire,
All the fierce throbbing of a pride
That flames like fire.

Give me the calm that Dante wrought
From sensual din;
The peace that errant Wolsey sought
From stalwart sin.
I seek repose upon Thy breast
With child-like prayer;
Oh let me find the heavenly rest
And mercy there!

If I have, in rebellious ways,
Proffered my life;

If I have filled my daring days
With worldly strife;
If I have shunned the narrow path
In crime to fall—
Lead me from th' abode of wrath
And pardon all!

Banished from Thee! where shall I find
For my poor soul
A safe retreat from storms that blind,
Or seas that roll?
Come to me, Christ, ere I, forlorn,
Sin 'neath the wave,
And on this blessed Easter morn
A lost one save!

James Ryder Randall

From "JESUS OF THE SCARS"

If we never sought, we seek Thee now;
Thine eyes burn through the dark, our only stars;
We must have sight of thorn-pricks on Thy brow,
We must have Thee, O Jesus of the Scars.

The heavens frighten us; they are too calm;
In all the universe we have no place.
Our wounds are hurting us; where is the balm?
Lord Jesus, by Thy Scars we claim Thy grace.

If when the doors are shut, Thou drawest near,
Only reveal those hands, that side of Thine;
We know today what wounds are, have no fear,
Show us Thy Scars, we know the countersign.

The other gods were strong; but Thou wast weak;
They rode, Thou didst stumble to a throne;
But to our wounds God's wounds alone can speak,
And not a god has wounds, but Thou alone.

Edward Shillito

"SWEET JESUS, IF IT BE THY WILL"

Sweet Jesu, if it be Thy will: unto my plaints attend;
Grant grace that I may continue still: Thy servant to the end.
Grant, blessed Lord, grant Saviour sweet: grant Jesu King of bliss,
That in Thy love I live and die: sweet Jesu, grant me this.

Anonymous

VENI CREATOR SPIRITUS

Creator Spirit, by whose aid
The world's foundations first were laid,
Come visit every pious mind,
Come pour thy joys on human-kind;
From sin and sorrow set us free,
And make thy temples worthy thee.

O source of uncreated light,
The Father's promised Paraclete!
Thrice holy fount, thrice holy fire,
Our hearts with heavenly love inspire;
Come, and thy sacred unction bring,
To sanctify us while we sing.

Plenteous of grace, descend from high,
Rich in thy seven-fold energy!
Thou strength of His Almighty hand,
Whose power does heaven and earth command!
Proceeding Spirit, our defense,
Who dost the gifts of tongues dispense,
And crown'st thy gift with eloquence!

Refine and purge our earthly parts;
But, O, inflame and fire our hearts!
Our frailties help, our vice control,
Submit the senses to the soul;
And when rebellious they are grown,
Then lay thy hand and hold them down.

Chase from our minds the infernal foe,
And peace, the fruit of love, bestow;
And, lest our feet should step astray,
Protect and guide us in the way.
Make us eternal truths receive,
And practice all that we believe;
Give us thyself, that we may see
The Father, and the Son, by thee.

Immortal honour, endless fame,
Attend the Almighty Father's name;
The Saviour Son be glorified,
Who for lost man's redemption died;
And equal adoration be,
Eternal Paraclete, to thee.

John Dryden

AT CONFIRMATION

Signed with the Cross that Jesus bore,
We kneel, and tremblingly adore
Our King upon His throne.
The lights upon the altar shine
Around His majesty divine,
Our God and Mary's Son.

Now, in that presence dread and sweet,
His own dear Spirit we entreat,
Who sevenfold gifts hath shed
On us, who fall before Him now,
Bearing the Cross upon our brow
On which our Master bled.

Henry A. Rawes

PENTECOSTAL HYMN

Holy Spirit, come upon us
With Thy Pentecostal Fire!

Bring us, sacred Dove celestial,
Vision of the World's Desire.

On the bitter Cross He suffered,
Leaving us immortal love,
Yet our hearts are lonely waiting
For the Comforter, the Dove.

Now we see the tongues descending!
Flaming tongues of power and light
Shine forever on our darkness,
Drive afar our faithless night.

Till, regathered in the sheepfold,
One, from many, we shall be,
As Thou art with Son and Father
In the Holy Trinity!

John Jerome Rooney

THE HOLY GHOST

O Holy Ghost, whose temple I
Am, but of muddy walls, and condensed dust,
And being sacrilegiously
Half wasted with youths fires, of pride and lust,
Must with new storms be weatherbeat;
Double in my heart thy flame,
Which let devout sad tears intend; and let
(Though this glass lanthorn, flesh, do suffer maim)
Fire, Sacrifice, Priest, Altar be the same.

John Donne

FOR CONFIRMATION

My God, accept my heart this day,
And make it always Thine,—

That I from Thee no more may stray,
No more from Thee decline.

* * * *

Anoint me with Thy heavenly grace,
Adopt me for Thine own,—
That I may see Thy glorious face,
And worship at Thy throne!

Madeline Bridges

FOR LIGHT AND GUIDANCE

"THY WORD IS A LAMP TO MY FEET"

Thy word is a lamp to my feet, and a light to my paths.
I have sworn and am determined to keep the judgments of thy justice.
I have been humbled, O Lord, exceedingly: quicken thou me according to thy word.
The free offerings of my mouth make acceptable, O Lord: and teach me thy judgments.

Psalm 118: 105–108

A PRAYER

God feed me understanding,
Bit by curious bit,
So that my tiny soul
Shall not be surfeited
With wonder.

A. M. Sullivan

PER PACEM AD LUCEM

I do not ask, O Lord, that life may be
  A pleasant road;
I do not ask that Thou wouldst take from me
  Aught of its load.

I do not ask that flowers should always spring
  Beneath my feet;
I know too well the poison and the sting
  Of things too sweet.

For one thing only, Lord, dear Lord, I plead,
  Lead me aright–
Though strength should falter, and though heart should bleed–
  Through Peace to Light.

I do not ask my cross to understand,
  My way to see;
Better in darkness just to feel Thy hand
  And follow Thee.

Joy is like restless day; but peace divine
  Like quiet night;
Lead me, O Lord,–till perfect Day shall shine,
  Through Peace to Light.

Adelaide Anne Procter

PRAYER FOR PERSEVERANCE

How many times, how many years
  This heart has cried the filial claim
To innocence untouched of tears
  And love beyond the reach of blame.

Still unappeased, the panting breast
  Can only crave a little sleep.
Eve's ancient fever will not rest,
  And Adam's malady is deep.

O Breath from Love's abyss! O balm!
  O Christ Who conquered hell's intrigue,
Sustain me. You have heard my psalm.
  You know the famine, the fatigue.

Clifford J. Laube

THE DARKNESS

Master of spirits! hear me: King of souls!
I kneel before Thine altar, the long night,
Besieging Thee with penetrable prayers;
And all I ask, light from the Face of God.
Thy darkness Thou has given me enough,
The dark clouds of Thine angry majesty:
Now give me light! I cannot always walk
Surely beneath the full and starless night.
Lighten me, fallen down, I know not where,
Save, to the shadows and the fear of death.
Thy Saints in light see light, and sing for joy:
Safe from the dark, safe from the dark and cold.
But from my dark comes only doubt of light:
Disloyalty, that trembles to despair.
Now bring me out of night, and with the sun
Clothe me, and crown me with Thy seven stars,
Thy spirits in the hollow of Thine hand.
Thou from the still throne of Thy tabernacle
Wilt come to me in glory, O Lord God!

Thou wilt, I doubt Thee not: I worship Thee
Before Thine holy altar, the long night.
Else have I nothing in the world, but death:
Thine hounding winds rush by me day and night,
Thy seas roar in mine ears: I have no rest,
No peace, but am afflicted constantly,
Driven from wilderness to wilderness.
And yet Thou hast a perfect house of light,
Above the four great winds, an house of peace:
Its beauty of the crystal and the dew,
Guard Angels and Archangels, in their hands
The blade of a sword shaken. Thither bring
Thy servant: when the black night falls on me,
With bitter voices tempting in the gloom,
Send out Thine armies, flaming ministers,
And shine upon the night: for what I would,
I cannot, save these help me. O Lord God!
Now, when my prayers upon Thine altar lie,
When Thy dark anger is too hard for me:
Through vision of Thyself, through flying fire,
Have mercy, and give light, and stablish me!

Lionel Johnson

*FIAT LUX**

"Give us this day our daily bread," and light;
  For more to me, O Lord, than food is sight:
    And I at noon have been
In twilight, where my fellow-men were seen
  "As trees" that walked before me. E'en today
From time to time there falls upon my way
  A feather of the darkness. But again
It passes; and amid the falling rain
  Of tears, I lift, O Lord, mine eyes to Thee,
    For, lo! I *see!*

John Banister Tabb

* Father Tabb was going blind at the time this was written.

THE PILLAR OF THE CLOUD

Lead, Kindly Light, amid the encircling gloom
  Lead Thou me on!
The night is dark, and I am far from home—
  Lead Thou me on!
Keep Thou my feet; I do not ask to see
The distant scene,—one step enough for me.

I was not ever thus, nor pray'd that Thou
  Shouldst lead me on.
I lov'd to choose and see my path; but now
  Lead Thou me on!
I lov'd the garish day, and, spite of fears,
Pride rul'd my will: remember not past years.

So long Thy power hath bless'd me, sure it still
  Will lead me on,
O'er moor and fen, o'er crag and torrent, till
  The night is gone;
And with the morn those angel faces smile
Which I have lov'd long since, and lost awhile.

John Henry Newman

"STRETCH FORTH THY HAND"

Thou art, O God, and in Thy holy light,
  I see that I too am, and am Thy child,
  Though weak and helpless and all sin-defiled,
Doing the wrong, while still I love the right.

But let I live always within Thy sight,
  And when I stray by vanities beguiled,
  Nor hearken to Thy pleadings sweet and mild,
Then most I feel Thy tender love's deep might.

Father! stretch forth Thy hand, up lift my mind,
  My heart and soul, and all that makes me man,
Pour forth Thy light, give sight to me purblind:
  Teach me of human life the perfect plan;

The scattered powers of all my being up-bind,
And be Thy love of death's dark stream the span.

John Lancaster Spalding

"WHY DOST THOU SHADE THY LOVELY FACE?"

Why dost thou shade thy lovely face? O why
Does that eclipsing hand so long deny
The sunshine of thy soul-enlivening eye?

Without that light, what light remains in me?
Thou art my life, my way, my light; in thee
I live, I move, and by thy beams I see. . . .

Thou art my way; I wander, if thou fly:
Thou art my light; if hid, how blind am I!
Thou art my life; if thou withdraw, I die.

Mine eyes are blind and dark, I cannot see;
To whom, or whither should my darkness flee,
But to the light? and who's that light but thee?

My path is lost, my wand'ring steps do stray;
I cannot safely go, nor safely stay;
Whom should I seek but thee, my path, my way? . . .

And yet thou turn'st away thy face, and fly'st me;
And yet I sue for grace, and thou deny'st me;
Speak, art thou angry, Lord, or only try'st me?

Unscreen those heav'nly lamps, or tell me why
Thou shad'st thy face: perhaps thou think'st no eye
Can view those flames, and not drop down and die.

If that be all, shine forth and draw me nigher;
Let me behold and die, for my desire
Is, phoenix-like, to perish in that fire.

Francis Quarles

A PRAYER

Often the western wind has sung to me,
There have been voices in the streams and meres,
And pitiful trees have told me, God, of Thee:
And I heard not. Oh! open Thou mine ears.

The reeds have whispered low as I passed by,
"Be strong, O friend, be strong, put off vain fears,
Vex not thy soul for doubts, God cannot lie":
And I heard not. Oh! open Thou mine ears.

There have been many stars to guide my feet,
Often the delicate moon, hearing my sighs,
Has rent the clouds and shown a silver street;
And I saw not. Oh! open Thou mine eyes.

Angels have beckoned me unceasingly,
And walked with me; and from the sombre skies
Dear Christ Himself has stretched out hands to me;
And I saw not. Oh! open Thou mine eyes.

Lord Alfred Douglas

From "AWAKE, MY SOUL"

Glory to Thee, who safe hast kept,
And hast refresh'd me whilst I slept:—
Grant, LORD, when I from death shall wake,
I may of endless light partake.

I would not wake, nor rise again,
E'en Heaven itself I would disdain,
Wert not Thou there to be enjoy'd,
And I in hymns to be employ'd.

Heaven is, dear LORD, where'er Thou art;
O never then from me depart;

For to my soul, 'tis hell to be,
But for one moment, without Thee.

LORD, I my vows to Thee renew,
Scatter my sins as morning dew;
Guard my first springs of thought and will,
And with Thyself my spirit fill.

Direct, control, suggest, this day,
All I design, or do, or say;
That all my powers, with all their might,
In Thy sole glory may unite.

Praise GOD, from whom all blessings flow,
Praise Him, all creatures here below;
Praise Him above, ye heavenly host,
Praise Father, Son, and Holy Ghost.

Thomas Ken

"ETERNAL WORD PROCEEDING FROM"

Eternal Word proceeding from
  The Heavenly Father's breast sublime,
Willing to help us Thou dost come
  In the appointed time.

Illumine now each waiting breast,
  Fill it with flames of Thy dear love,
That in our hearts alone may rest
  Desire of joys above.

That when to flames the Judgment Seat
  Condemns the bad for evil done,
And calls the just in accents sweet
  Unto their Heaven won;

We may not feed the hungry flame
  Tossed in the black and whirling pool,

But rather God's great Presence claim
In heavenly pastures cool.

Unto the Father and the Son
And Spirit Paraclete, to Thee
What praise hath been, so be it done
Through all eternity.

Saint Ambrose (translated by H. T. Henry)

"I HAVE CRIED TO THEE, O LORD"

I have cried to thee, O Lord, hear me: hearken to my voice, when I cry to thee.
Let my prayer be directed as incense in thy sight; the lifting up of my hands, as evening sacrifice.
Set a watch, O Lord, before my mouth: and a door round about my lips.
Incline not my heart to evil words: to make excuses in sins.

Psalm 140:1–4

"O THOU WHO ART OUR AUTHOR AND OUR END"

O Thou Who art our Author and our End,
On Whose large mercy chains of hope depend;
Lift me to Thee by Thy propitious hand:
For lower I can find no place to stand.

Sir John Beaumont

THE UNIVERSAL PRAYER

Father of All! in ev'ry Age,
In ev'ry Clime ador'd,
By Saint, by Savage, and by Sage,
Jehovah, Jove, or Lord!

Thou Great First Cause, least understood:
Who all my Sense confin'd

To know but this, that Thou art Good,
  And that myself am blind;

Yet gave me, in this dark Estate,
  To see the Good from Ill;
And binding Nature fast in Fate,
  Let free the Human Will.

What Conscience dictates to be done,
  Or warns me not to do,
This, teach me more than Hell to shun,
  That, more than Heav'n pursue.

What Blessings thy free Bounty gives,
  Let me not cast away;
For God is pay'd when Man receives,
  To enjoy is to obey.

Yet not to Earth's contracted Span
  Thy Goodness let me bound,
Or think Thee Lord alone of Man,
  When thousand Worlds are round:

Let not this weak, unknowing hand
  Presume thy bolts to throw,
And deal damnation round the land,
  On each I judge thy Foe.

If I am right, thy grace impart,
  Still in the right to stay;
If I am wrong, oh teach my heart
  To find that better way.

Save me alike from foolish Pride,
  Or impious Discontent,
At aught thy Wisdom has deny'd,
  Or aught thy Goodness lent.

Teach me to feel another's Woe,
  To hide the Fault I see;

That Mercy I to others show,
  That Mercy show to me.

Mean tho' I am, not wholly so,
  Since quick'ned by thy Breath;
Oh lead me wheresoe'er I go,
  Thro' this day's Life or Death.

This day, be Bread and Peace my Lot:
  All else beneath the Sun,
Thou know'st if best bestow'd or not;
  And let Thy Will be done.

To thee, whose Temple is all Space,
  Whose Altar Earth, Sea, Skies,
One Chorus let all Being raise,
  All Nature's Incense rise!

Alexander Pope

"GIVE NOT TO ME, O GOD, MY HEART'S DESIRE"

Give not to me, O God, my heart's desire,
  For I am blind and know not what is best,
  More than a babe asleep on mother's breast,
But do Thy will: Uplift Thy children higher.

Nearer to Thee, from out the soil and mire,
  Of selfish loves in which no man is blest,
  Lead me on their wandering steps to where is rest,
In sight of Thee to whom all hearts aspire.

This is my prayer, this is the yearning deep
  Of my true self, for in the good of all
The good of each is found; therefore I keep
  My thoughts above myself and am Thy thrall;
Thy servant in Thy fields Thy grain I reap,
  And have no hope save in Thy mercy's call.

John Lancaster Spalding

"LORD, SPEAK TO ME, THAT I MAY SPEAK"

Lord, speak to me, that I may speak
  In living echoes of Thy tone;
As Thou hast sought, so let me seek
  Thy erring children lost and lone.

O teach me, Lord, that I may teach
  The precious things Thou dost impart;
And wing my words, that they may reach
  The hidden depths of many a heart.

O fill me with Thy fullness, Lord,
  Until my very heart o'erflow
In kindling thought and glowing word,
  Thy love to tell, Thy praise to show.

O use me, Lord, use even me,
  Just as Thou wilt, and when and where;
Until Thy blessed face I see,
  Thy rest, Thy joy, Thy glory share.

Frances Ridley Havergal

From THE LITANY

From being anxious, or secure,
  Dead clods of sadness, or light squibs of mirth,
  From thinking, that great courts immure
All, or no happiness, or that this earth
    Is only for our prison fram'd,
    Or that thou art covetous
To them whom thou lovest, or that they are maim'd
From reaching this world's sweet, who seek thee thus,
With all their might, Good Lord deliver us.

  From needing danger, to be good,
From owing thee yesterday's tears today,
  From trusting so much to thy blood,

That in that hope, we wound our soul away,
From bribing thee with alms, to excuse
Some sin more burdenous,
From light affecting, in religion, news,
From thinking us all soul, neglecting thus
Our mutual duties, Lord deliver us. . . .

That we may change to evenness
This intermitting anguish piety;
That snatching cramps of wickedness
And apoplexies of fast sin, may die;
That music of thy promises,
Not threats in thunder may
Awaken us to our just offices;
What in thy book, thou dost, or creatures say,
That we may hear, Lord hear us, when we pray.

John Donne

TO THE CHRIST CHILD

Teach, O teach us, holy Child,
By Thy face so meek and mild,
Teach us to resemble Thee,
In Thy sweet humility!
Hail, Thou ever-blessed morn!
Hail, redemption's happy dawn!
Sing through all Jerusalem,
Christ is born in Bethlehem.

Edward Caswall

"LEAD ME TO THY PEACEFUL MANGER"

Lead me to Thy peaceful manger,
Wond'rous Babe of Bethlehem;
Shepherds hail Thee, yet a stranger;
Let me worship Thee with them.
I am vile, but Thou art holy;
Oh, unite my heart to Thee;

Make me contrite, keep me lowly,
Pure as Thou wouldst have me be.

Madeline Bridges

A PRAYER IN PRISON

O ever living Lord of lords,
O mighty King of kings,
O solace of the sorrowful,
O glass, who gladness brings:
O puissant Prince, O passing Power,
O Regent of all rule,
My guide, my guard, expel from me
All foolish fear and dule.

* * * *

Let not my sins me cause, O Lord,
To wander from the rock,
But grant I may be found in fold
Of Thine afflicted flock.

* * * *

As is Thy Holy Ghost, O Lord,
I pray that Thou wouldst spare,
The workers of my web of woe,
The causers of my care:
I humbly Thee beseech O Lord,
Even by Thy blessed blood,
Forgive their guilt, forgive their ill,
And send them all much good:
Turn not, O Lord, Thy face from me
Although a wretched wight,
But let me joy in Thee all day,
Rejoice in Thee all night.

* * * *

That after stirring storms are stayed,
And surging seas do cease,

I may with mirth cast anchor in,
The pleasant port of peace.

Francis Tregian

From HYMN TO CHRIST THE SAVIOUR

O Jesus, hear!
Shepherd and Sower, Thou,
Now helm, and bridle now,
Wing for the heavenward flight
Of flocks all pure and bright,
Fisher of men, the blest,
Out of the world's unrest,
Out of Sin's troubled sea
Taking us, Lord to Thee;
Out of the waves of strife
With bait of blissful life,
With choicest fish, good store,
Drawing Thy nets to shore.
Lead us. O Shepherd true,
Thy mystic sheep, we sue,
Lead us, Oh holy Lord,
Whom from Thy sons dost ward
With all-prevailing charm,
Peril, curse and harm;
O path where Christ has trod,
O way that leads to God,
O word abiding aye,
O endless Light on high,
Mercy's fresh-spring flood,
Worker of all things good,
O glorious Life of all
That on their Maker call.
Christ Jesus, hear! . . .
Our holy tribute, this,
For wisdom, life and bliss,
Singing in chorus meet,
Singing in concert sweet
The Almighty Son.

We, heirs of peace unpriced,
We, who are born in Christ,
A people pure from stain,
Praise we our God again,
Lord of our Peace!

Clement or Alexandria (translated by E. H. Plumtre)

SEND ME

O Thou best gift from Heaven,
Thou who Thyself hast given,
For Thou hast died–

This hast Thou done for me,–
What have I done for Thee,
Thou crucified?

I long to serve Thee more,
Reveal an open door
Saviour, to me.

Then counting all but loss,
I'll glory in Thy cross,
And follow Thee.

Anonymous

A BETTER RESURRECTION

I have no wit, no words, no tears;
My heart within me like a stone
Is numbed too much for hopes or fears;
Look right, look left, I dwell alone;
I lift mine eyes, but dimmed with grief
No everlasting hills I see;
My life is in the falling leaf:
O Jesus, quicken me.

My life is like a faded leaf,
My harvest dwindled to a husk;
Truly my life is void and brief
And tedious in the barren dusk;
My life is like a frozen thing,
No bud nor greenness can I see:
Yet rise it shall—the sap of Spring;
O Jesus, rise in me.

My life is like a broken bowl,
A broken bowl that cannot hold
One drop of water for my soul
Or cordial in the searching cold;
Cast in the fire the perished thing,
Melt and remould it, till it be
A royal cup for Him my King
O Jesus, drink of me.

Christina Rossetti

LINES

I cannot soar and sing my Lord and love;
No eagle's wings have I,
No power to rise and greet my King above,
No heart to fly.
Creative Lord Incarnate, let me lean
My heavy self on Thee;
Nor let my utter weakness come between
Thy strength and me.

I cannot trace Thy Providence and plan,
Nor dimly comprehend
What in Thyself Thou art, and what is man,
And what the end.
Here in the wilderness I cannot find
The path the Wise Men trod;
Grant me to rest on Thee, Incarnate Mind
And Word of God.

I cannot love, my heart is turned within
   And locked within; (Ah me!
How shivering in self-love I sit) for sin
   Has lost the key.
Ah! Sacred Heart of Jesus, Flame divine,
   Ardent with great desire,
My hope is set upon that love of Thine,
   Deep Well of Fire.

I cannot live alone another hour;
   Jesu, be Thou my Life!
I have not power to strive; be Thou my Power
   In every strife!
I can do nothing—hope, nor love, nor fear,
   But only fail and fall.
Be Thou my soul and self, O Jesu dear,
   My God and All!

Robert Hugh Benson

"GIVE ME, O CHRIST, A MILD AND LOWLY HEART"

Give me, O Christ, a mild and lowly heart,
   That from all vain desires I may find rest,
   And taste the peace that dwells within Thy heart,
And learn of happy life the simple art;

So in Thy kingdom I may have a part,
   And at Thy feast be not unwelcome guest
   With loving Mary who chose well the best,
Made wise by perfect love and sin's deep smart.

Teach me to walk in humbleness and fear,
   And ever close to Thee like a meek child
Who in dark place keeps to its mother near,
   When passion's storms are loud and wild,
Within my soul let me Thy calm voice hear,
   Speaking the "Peace—be still" in accent mild.

John Lancaster Spalding

PRAYER TO THE BLESSED VIRGIN

Fire of heaven's eternal ray
　Gentle and unscorching flame,
Strength in moments of dismay,
　Grief's redress and sorrow's balm,—
Light thy servant on his way!
Teach him all earth's passing folly,
　All its dazzling art
　　To distrust;
And let thoughts profound and holy
　Penetrate his heart
　　Low in dust.
Lead him to the realms sublime
　Where thy footsteps tread;
　Teach him, Virgin! so to dread
Judgment's soul-tormenting clime,
That he may harvest for the better time.

Rodríguez De Padrón (translated by John Bowring)

O MARY OF GRACES

O Mary of Graces
　And Mother of God,
May I tread in the paths
　That the righteous have trod.

And mayst thou save me
　From evil's control,
And mayst thou save me
　In body and soul.

And mayst thou save me
　By land and by sea,
And mayst thou save me
　From tortures to be.

May the guard of the angels
　Above me abide,

May God be before me
And God at my side.

Anonymous (translated from the Gaelic by Douglas Hyde)

TO OUR LADY

Hail Mary, pearl of grace,
Pure flower of Adam's race,
And vessel rare of God's election;
Unstained as virgin snow,
Serene as sunset glow—
We sinners crave thy sure protection.

Thou Queen of high estate,
Conceived immaculate
To form incarnate Love's pure dwelling;
The spirit found His rest
Within thy sinless breast,
And thence flows joy beyond all telling.

* * * *

Through His dear blood Who died,
By sinners crucified,
Art thou preserved, and we forgiven,
Help us to conquer sin,
That we may enter in,
Through thee, the golden gate, to heaven.

Dom Bede Camm

A DAILY HYMN TO MARY

Mary! Dearest Mother!
From thy heavenly height
Look on us thy children,
Lost in earth's dark night.

Mary! purest creature!
Keep us all from sin;

Help us erring mortals
Peace in heaven to win.

Mary! Queen and Mother!
Get us still more grace,
With still greater fervor
Now to run our race.

Daughter of the Father!
Lady kind and sweet!
Lead up to our Father,
Leave us at His Feet.

Mother of our Saviour,
Joy of God above!
Jesus bade tnee keep us
In His fear and love.

Mary! Spouse and servant
Of the Holy Ghost!
Keep for Him His creatures
Who would else be lost.

Holy Queen of angels!
Bid thine angels come
To escort us safely
To our heavenly home.

Bid the saints in heaven
Pray for us their prayers;
They are thine, dear Mother!
That thou mayst be theirs.

Oh, we love thee, Mary!
Trusting all to thee,
What is past, or present,
What is yet to be.

Get us what thou pleasest,
What we cannot know,

What we most are needing
  Every day below.

Thou didst make for Jesus
  To this earth a road;
Make us love our Saviour,
  Make us love our God.

Cause of all our gladness!
  Make us glad in Him;
Fill our hearts with fervor,
  Fill them to the brim.

Sweeter still and sweeter
  Dost thou grow to us,—
Will it, dearest Mother,
  Evermore be thus?

O not yet, sweet Mother!
  Is our love of thee
What it will be one day
  In eternity.

Jesus! hear thy children
  From Thy throne above;
Give us love of Mary,
  As thou wouldst have us love.

Frederick W. Faber

MEA CULPA

Be pitiful, my God!
  No hard-won gifts I bring—
But empty, pleading hands
  To Thee at evening.

Spring came, white-browed and young,
  I, too, was young with Spring.

There was a blue, blue heaven
  Above a skylark's wing.

Youth is the time for joy,
  I cried, it is not meet
To mount the heights of toil
  With child-soft feet.

When Summer walked the land
  In Passion's red arrayed,
Under green sweeping boughs
  My couch I made.

The noon-tide heat was sore,
  I slept the Summer through;
An angel waked me—"Thou
  Hast work to do."

I rose and saw the sheaves
  Upstanding in a row;
The reapers sang Thy praise
  While passing to and fro.

My hands were soft with ease,
  Long were the Autumn hours;
I left the ripened sheaves
  For poppy-flowers.

But lo! now Winter glooms,
  And gray is in my hair,
Whither has flown the world
  I found so fair?

My patient God, forgive!
  Praying Thy pardon sweet
I lay a lonely heart
  Before Thy feet.

Ethna Carberry

HYMN TO GOD THE FATHER

Hear me, O God!
  A broken heart
  Is my best part:
Use still Thy rod,
  That I may prove
  Therein, my love.

If thou hadst not
  Been stern to me,
  But left me free,
I had forgot
  Myself and thee.

For sin's so sweet,
  As minds ill bent
  Rarely repent,
Until they meet
  Their punishment.

Who more can crave
  Than thou hast done:
  That gav'st a Son,
To free a slave?
  First made of nought;
  With all since bought.

Sin, Death, and Hell,
  His glorious Name
  Quite overcame;
Yet I rebel,
  And slight the same.

But I'll come in,
  Before my loss,
  Me farther toss,
As sure to win
  Under His Cross.

Ben Jonson

"VIEW ME, LORD, A WORK OF THINE"

View me, Lord, a work of thine:
Shall I then lie drown'd in night?
Might thy grace in me but shine,
I should seem made all of light.

But my soul still surfeits so
On the poised baits of sin,
That I strange and ugly grow,
All is dark and foul within.

Cleanse me, Lord, that I may kneel
At thine altar, pure and white:
They that once they mercies feel,
Gaze no more on earth's delight.

Worldly joys like shadows fade,
When the heav'nly light appears;
But the cov'nants thou hast made,
Endless, know not days, nor years.

In thy word, Lord, is my trust,
To thy mercies fast I fly;
Though I am but clay and dust,
Yet thy grace can lift me high.

Thomas Campion

GOOD FRIDAY

Am I a stone, and not a sheep,
  That I can stand, O Christ, beneath Thy cross,
  To number drop by drop Thy Blood's slow loss,
And yet not weep?

Not so those women loved
  Who with exceeding grief lamented Thee;
  Not so fallen Peter weeping bitterly;
Not so the thief was moved;

Not so the Sun and Moon
Which hid their faces in a starless sky.
A horror of great darkness at broad noon—
I, only I.

Yet give not o'er
But seek Thy sheep, true Shepherd of the flock;
Greater than Moses, turn and look once more
And smite a rock.

Christina Rossetti

PRAYER OF A SOLDIER IN FRANCE

My shoulders ache beneath the pack
(Lie easier, Cross, upon His back).

I march with feet that burn and smart
(Tread, Holy Feet, upon my heart).

Men shout at me who may not speak
(They scourged Thy back and smote Thy cheek).

I may not lift a hand to clear
My eyes of salty drops that sear.

(Then shall my fickle soul forget
Thy Agony of Bloody Sweat?).

My rifle hand is stiff and numb
(From Thy pierced palm red rivers come).

Lord, Thou didst suffer more for me
Than all the hosts of land and sea.

So, let me render back again
This millionth of Thy gift. Amen.

Joyce Kilmer

VIGILS

Once I knelt in my shining mail
   Here by Thine altar all the night.
My heart beat proudly, my prayer rose loudly,
   But I looked to my armor to win the fight.

God, my lance was a broken reed,
   My mace a toy for a child's delight.
My helmet is battered, my shield is shattered,
   I am stiff with wounds, and I lost the fight.

Lord I kneel through the night again,
   Hear my prayer, if my prayer be right!
Take for Thy token my proud heart broken.
   God guide my arm! I go back to the fight!

Aline Kilmer

"GRANT, I PRAY THEE"

Grant, I pray Thee, such heat into mine heart
That to this love of Thine may be equal;
Grant me from Satan's service to astart,
With whom me rueth so lone to have be thrall;
Grant me, good Lord and Creator of all,
The flame to quench of all sinful desire
And in Thy love set all mine heart afire;

That when the journey of this deadly life
My silly ghost hath finishèd, and thence
Departen must without his fleshly wife,
Alone into his Lordès high presence,
He may Thee find, O well of indulgence,
In Thy lordship not as a lord, but rather
As a very tender loving father.

Picco Della Mirandola (translated by St. Thomas More)

From THE LITANY

Hear us, O hear us Lord; to thee
A sinner is more music, when he prays,
Than spheres, or Angels' praises be,
In Panegyric Allelujas;
Hear us, for till thou hear us, Lord
We know not what to say;
Thine ear to our sighs, tears, thoughts gives voice and word.
O Thou who Satan heard'st in Job's sick day,
Hear thy self now, for thou in us dost pray.

* * * *

Son of God hear us, and since thou
By taking our blood, owest it to us again,
Gain to thy self, or us allow;
And let not both us and thy self be slain;
O Lamb of God, which took'st our sin
Which could not stick to thee,
O let it not return to us again,
But Patient and Physician being free,
As sin is nothing, let it no where be.

John Donne

LUX ADVENIT VENERANDA

Thou whose prayer doth vice destroy,
Thou whose name brings only joy,
Thou whose perfume shames the rose,
Thou whose lip with nectar flows
Sweeter than the honeycomb;
Redder than the rose art thou,
Whiter than the falling snow,
Dewier than the rose dew-strewn,
Brighter than the splendrous moon
Shinest thou in heaven's dome.
Empress of the host supernal,
Victress over foes infernal,
Pathway leading up to heaven
To be followed as 'twas given;

Call them back who far have wandered,
And, recalled, what they have squandered—
Show them how it may be won!
To thy clients thee addressing
Grant in fullness every blessing;
Nor the lowly sinner spurning,
But his pleading heart discerning;
And thus all who feel their weakness
And beseech thy loving meekness
Place before thy pardoning Son!

Adam of St. Victor (translated by H. T. Henry)

OUR LADY OF THE REFUGEES

Mother who knew
what hardship shakes
a woman bundling clothes,
and putting by her wheaten cakes;
Mother who urged the donkey,
(making happy riot
on the straggling stones)
urged the beast to be more quiet;
Mother who heard the Child
whimper beneath the thin blue shawl,
our aching prayers cry out to thee,
Mother, pray for them all.

A thousand Bethlehems
mask dark tonight,
the eyes of friendly little homes
have lost their light;
pathetic heaps of poor, dear things
are laid aside; a small bird sang
where a latched door swings.
Mother, whose sad Egyptian flight
preceded all of these
guide them in faith beneath familiar stars,
Our Lady of the Refugees.

Sister Mary Maura

IMMACULATE PALM

Beautiful, Beautiful Mother, give
from your Immaculate Palm
a soothing, healing unseen balm
for boys who want to live.

Holiest, Holiest Mother, take
from the enveloping night
the sick boy's weeping for the light,
and whisper softly, "Wake."

Sorrowful, Sorrowful Mother, lift
salve that is borrowed above
for pierced ones. Let them feel His love,
and lead them out of tomb-like mind
where dwell believing blind,
You, who gave your Precious Gift.

Joseph Joel Keith

LADY OF THE LILACS

Lovely Lady of the Lilacs,
  Clothed in robes of flowing stone,
Set a guard around this lad:
  Never let him walk alone.

Once You soothed a sobbing Boy
  Frightened in the shades of night.
Take this other son to you:
  Guard him . . . guide him in the right.

Your First-Born loved you deeply-well,
  Treasured high your tender heart.
May this other love thee too:
  From thee never be apart.

William Noé Field

PENITENCE AND PARDON

"OUT OF THE DEPTHS I HAVE CRIED"

Out of the depths I have cried to thee, O Lord: Lord, hear my voice.
Let thy ears be attentive to the voice of my supplication.
If thou, O Lord, wilt mark iniquities: Lord, who shall stand it.
For with thee there is merciful forgiveness: and by reason of thy law,
I have waited for thee, O Lord.
My soul hath relied on his word: my soul hath hoped in the Lord.

Psalm 129:1–5

PRODIGAL

Like a bird that trails a broken wing,
  I have come home to Thee;
Home from a flight and freedom
  That was never meant for me.

And I, who have known far spaces,
  And the fierce heat of the sun,
Ask only the shelter of Thy wings,
  Now that the day is done.

Like a bird that trails a broken wing,
  I have come home, at last. . . .
O hold me to Thy Heart once more,
  And hide me from the past.

Ellen Gilbert

A HYMN TO GOD THE FATHER

Wilt Thou forgive that sin where I begun;
  Which was my sin, though it were done before?
Wilt Thou forgive that sin through which I run,
  And do run still, though still I do deplore?
When Thou has done, Thou hast not done;
  For I have more.

Wilt Thou forgive that sin which I have won
  Others to sin, and made my sins their door?
Wilt Thou forgive that sin which I did shun
  A year or two, but wallowed in, a score?
When Thou has done, Thou hast not done:
  For I have more.

I have a sin of fear, that when I've spun
  My last thread, I shall perish on the shore;
But swear by Thyself that at my death Thy Son
  Shall shine as He shines now, and heretofore;

And having done that, Thou hast done;
I fear no more.

John Donne

THE SINS OF YOUTH

Thou that didst grant the wise King his request,
Thou that in whale thy prophet didst preserve:
Thou that forgavest the wounding of thy breast,
Thou that didst save the thief in state to serve.
Thou only God, the giver of all grace,
Wipe out of mind, the path of youth's vain race.

Thou that by power, to life didst raise the dead,
Thou that of grace restorest the blind to sight;
Thou that for love, thy life and love outbled:
Thou that of favor, madest the lame go right,
Thou that canst heal, and help in all assays
Forgive the guilt, that grew in youth's vain ways.

Thomas Vaux

FOR INTERCESSION

Hail, Queen of Heav'n, the ocean star,
Guide of the wand'rer here below:
Thrown on life's surge, we claim thy care—
Save us from peril and from woe.
Mother of Christ, Star of the Sea,
Pray for the wanderer, pray for me.

O gentle, chaste, and spotless Maid,
We sinners make our prayers through thee;
Remind thy Son that He has paid
The price of our iniquity.
Virgin most pure, Star of the Sea,
Pray for the sinner, pray for me.

John Lingard

THE NIGHTINGALE

As the mute nightingale in closest groves
  Lies hid at noon, but when day's piercing eye
  Is locked in night, with full heart beating high
Poured forth her plain-son o'er the light she loves;
So, Virgin Ever-pure and Ever-blest,
  Moon of religion, from whose radiant face,
  Reflected, streams the light of heavenly grace
On broken hearts, by contrite thoughts oppressed;
So, Mary, they who justly feel the weight
  Of Heaven's offended Majesty, implore
  Thy reconciling aid with suppliant knee:
Of sinful man, O sinless Advocate,
  To thee they turn, nor Him they less adore;
    'Tis still His light they love, less dreadful seen in thee.

Gerald Griffin

"TIMES WITHOUT NUMBER HAVE I PRAY'D"

Times without number have I pray'd,
  "This only once forgive";
Relapsing, when Thy hand was stay'd,
  And suffer'd me to live:—

Yet now the kingdom of Thy peace,
  LORD, to my heart restore;
Forgive my vain repentances,
  And bid me sin no more.

Charles Wesley

From *STABAT MATER*

Fount of love and sacred sorrow,
Mother, may my spirit borrow
  Sadness from thy holy woe;
May it love—on fire within me—

Christ, my God, till great love win me
   Grace to please him here below.

Those five wounds of Jesus smitten,
Mother, in my heart be written
   Deeply as in thine they be;
Thou my Savior's cross who bearest,
Thou thy Son's rebuke who sharest,
   Let me share them both with thee.

In the passion of my maker
Be my sinful soul partaker;
   Let me weep till death with thee:
Unto me this boon be given,
By thy side, like thee bereaven,
   To stand beneath the atoning tree.

Virgin holiest, Virgin purest,
Of that anguish thou endurest
   Make me bear with thee my part;
Of his passion bear the token
In a spirit bowed and broken,
   Bear his death within my heart.

May his wounds both wound and heal me;
His blood enkindle, cleanse, anneal me;
   Be his cross my hope and stay:
Virgin, when the mountains quiver,
From that flame which burns for ever,
   Shield me on the judgment-day.

Christ, when he that shaped me calls me,
When advancing death appals me,
   Through her prayer the storm make calm:
When to dust my dust returneth
Save a soul to thee that yearneth;
   Grant it thou the crown and palm.

Jacapone Da Todi (translated by Aubrey De Vere)

"O SACRED HEAD, NOW WOUNDED"

O sacred Head, now wounded,
With grief and shame weighed down,
Now scornfully surrounded
With thorns, Thy only crown,
How art Thou pale with anguish,
With sore abuse and scorn!
How does that visage languish
Which once was bright as morn!

What Thou, my Lord, hast suffered
Was all for sinners' gain:
Mine, mine was the transgression,
But Thine the deadly pain.
Lo, here I fall, my Saviour!
'Tis I deserve Thy place;
Look on me with Thy favor,
Vouchsafe to me Thy grace.

What language shall I borrow,
To thank Thee, dearest Friend,
For this Thy dying sorrow,
Thy pity without end?
O make me Thine forever;
And, should I fainting be,
Lord, let me never, never,
Outlive my love to Thee!

Ascribed to Arnulf von Loewen (translated by James Alexander)

O THAT I HAD WINGS LIKE A DOVE

O Gracious God, O Saviour sweet,
  O Jesus, think on me,
And suffer me to kiss Thy feet,
  Though late I come to Thee.

Behold, dear LORD, I come to Thee
  With sorrow and with shame,

For when Thy bitter wounds I see,
  I know I caused the same.

Sweet JESU, who shall lend me wings
  Of peace and perfect love,
That I may rise from earthly things
  To rest with Thee above?

For sin and sorrow overflow
  All earthly things so high,
That I can find no rest below,
  But unto Thee I fly.

Wherefore my soul doth loathe the things
  Which gave it once delight,
And unto Thee, the King of kings,
  Would mount with all her might.

And yet the weight of flesh and blood
  Doth so my wings restrain,
That oft I strive and gain no good,
  But rise, to fall again.

Yet when this fleshly misery
  Is master'd by the mind,
I cry, "Avaunt, all vanity":
  And "Satan, stand behind."

So thus, sweet LORD, I fly about
  In weak and weary case
Like the lone dove which Noah sent out,
  And found no resting place.

My weary wings, sweet JESU, mark,
  And when Thou thinkest best
Stretch forth Thy arm from out the ark,
  And take me to Thy rest.

Anonymous

CONTRITION

Plead Thou my cause; yet let me bear the pain,
Lord, Who hast done so much to ransome me,
Now that I know how I have wounded Thee,
And crucified Thee, Prince of Life, again.
Yea, let me suffer; Thou wilt not disdain
To let me hang beside Thee on the Tree
And taste Thy bitter Cup of agony.
Let it not be that Thou hast died in vain.

Ah, awful Face of Love, bruised by my hand,
Turn to me, pierce me with Thine eye of flame,
And give me deeper knowledge of my sin.
So let me grieve; and, when I understand
How great my guilt, my ruin, and my shame,
Open Thy Sacred Heart and let me in!

Robert Hugh Benson

WALL CRUCIFIX

Be thou, in all my falling,
O figure of fastened pain!
A soft compassionate calling
Over my anguished brain.

Hung there in moveless dying
A twist of oak like a groan,
Hear thou the choke of my crying
That seeks to atone.

Be thou my kind reprieving,
My strength to rise from the dirt
And face thee, grieving for grieving
God that I humbled and hurt.

But not to thy face, O Master,
My eyes are lifted to greet,

But fixed on the speechless disaster
That stares in Thy tortured feet.

Thy face is unbearable chiding
I flee to the refuge of bone
Too broken for sparing or striding
And stiller than stone.

John Duffy

FORGIVENESS

O heart of Jesus, purest heart,
Altar of holiness Thou art,
Cleanse Thou my heart, so sordid, cold,
And stained by sins so manifold.

Take from me, Lord, this tepid will,
Which doth Thy heart with loathing fill;
And then infuse a spirit new—
A fervent spirit, deep and true.

Anonymous (translated by Matthew Russell)

TOMORROW

Lord, what am I, that, with unceasing care,
  Thou did'st seek after me, that thou did'st wait,
  Wet with unhealthy dews, before my gate,
And pass the gloomy nights of winter there?
Oh, strange delusion, that I did not greet
  Thy blest approach! and oh, to heaven how lost
  If my ingratitude's unkindly frost
Has chilled the bleeding wounds upon thy feet!

How oft my guardian angel gently cried,
  "Soul, from thy casement look, and thou shalt see
  How he persists to knock and wait for thee!"
    And oh! how often to that voice of sorrow,

"Tomorrow we will open," I replied,
And when the morrow came I answered still
"Tomorrow."

Lope de Vega (translated by H. W. Longfellow)

CONFESSION

I've bowed my head at last,
And I had held it high;
For pride, so great in past
Was very loath to die.

And now my will be Thine
I've learned through bitter loss,
That prouder heads than mine
Have bent to kiss the Cross.

Helen R. Kahn

RELUCTANT PRODIGAL

I know that Thou hast never turned from me,
I know that Thou hast never let me go;
That when I am most ignorant of Thee,
Thou art more near than whiteness is to snow!
But I have followed close upon the wind,
Regarding not the compass and the star;
In blinded ways and devious, have sinned;
Have made my fate of shattered mast and spar.

I cannot yet in formal penance kneel
Among the throng by daily habit led;
But let me to the outer edges steal
Of that great light from which Thy throne is shed;
My slow redemption having thus begun,
Be as a seedling working toward the sun.

Ernestine Parsons

PLAYING WITH FIRE

Pardon us, Lord, when we play with fire,
For fire is a winsome thing:
Its glow outglories the fairest gem
In the crown of the proudest king.

It laughs and it leaps upon our hearth
While the earth lies sleeping in snow,
And set in a candle, it carries light
To the darkest corner we go.

It is life, it is love, it is ecstasy,
And it coaxes our gold from the dross—
Remind us not of the fields burned dry
Or the cities bowed black in loss!

Nay, turn Thy face and forget to chide
If our foolish fingers grow bold;
Pardon us, Lord, when we play with fire—
For our hands—and our hearts—are cold.

Katherine Brégy

DISTRACTION

When swarms of small distractions harry
Devotion like the gnats that fly
Till prayers are cold and customary
Not such as please Thee, Heaven-high:

When I forget for all my striving
Thy presence holy and august;
Be Thou not angry, but forgiving
To her Thou madest from the dust.

Say to Thyself: This mortal being,
So deaf, so blind, so prone to sin,
Hath glimpses of Me without seeing
The places where the nails went in.

Say, through the crusts of earth, My creature
Perceiving Me, hails Me Lord above.
Rumors of the lost innocence reach her
With full assurance of My love.

Say: of all marvels I have fashioned
Is none more wonderful and new
Than that this soul should go impassioned
For heights beyond her mortal view.

What though her weary mind should ponder
On small things meet for such as she,
O love! O loyalty! O wonder!
That in the darkness gropes for Me!

Katharine Tynan Hinkson

"TARDY WE COME TO THY MANSIONS, O LORD"

Tardy we come to Thy mansions, O Lord, having dulled our wits in the maze of the doubter.

Maimed and blind we stumble before Thee, asking solace of light, the fragrance of love, and chrism of grace.

Empty and cheated, we grovel before Thee, naked of pride, and eager for crumbs of Thy table.

We who have fouled the spring with the image of greed hold a leprous heart for Thy altar.

Unworthy we stand and clamor for healing waters, picking the scabs of the soul to hurry Thy mercy.

Isiah's lips were cleansed with a burning coal and Thy Breath was wind in the bellows.

Our lips were silenced with ice, a frosty blade that was forged by Thy breath against pride.

Lucifer sinned by the strength of the will, Adam by weakness of flesh,—
Woe to the angels:

Cold is Thy brand to the dueling mind that sins with whetted daggers of reason;

Blest me Thy hand that is warm on the penitent brow of him who burns and bleeds for his anger.

Holy thy tongue that pledged the height of the heavens to Golgotha's thief who reached for Thy mercy.

A. M. Sullivan

TO JESUS IN THE BLESSED SACRAMENT

"I HAVE LOVED, O LORD, THE BEAUTY OF THY HOUSE"

I have loved, O Lord, the beauty of thy house; and the place where thy glory dwelleth. . . .
My foot hath stood in the direct way: in the churches I will bless thee, O Lord.

Psalm 25:8, 12

OFFERTORY
(A Nun Speaks)

Thy priest, O Lord, the paten lifts on high—
The altar lights strain upward, and the Host
Is offered! 'neath Thine ever watchful eye.
Humbly I join to this dread sacrifice
My little life, its bitter and its sweet,
Laying each word and deed down at Thy feet.

And now that sacred chalice bears aloft
Its mystic weight of water and of wine:
Thou comest, Lord—surely Thy footsteps soft
Draw near to earth . . . And make me wholly Thine!
Teach me no thought nor dream to keep apart,
Be Thine the hopes, the love of all my heart.

Katherine Brégy

THE OFFERING

The bread that would Thine offering be
  Must lose its substance, changed to Thee!
I take the symbol, Lord, and fain
Would die—to live in Thee again.

Edward F. Garesché

TANTUM ERGO

Down in adoration falling,
  Lo! the Sacred Host we hail!
Lo, o'er ancient forms departing,
  Newer rites of grace prevail;
Faith for all defects supplying,
  Where the feeble senses fail.

To the Everlasting Father,
  And the Son who reigns on high,

With the Holy Ghost proceeding
  Forth from each eternally,
Be salvation, honor, blessing,
  Might and endless majesty!

St. Thomas Aquinas (translated by Edward Caswall)

LINES TO THE BLESSED SACRAMENT

Thou dear and mystic semblance,
  Before whose form I kneel,
I tremble as I think upon
  The glory thou dost veil,
And ask myself, can he who late
  The ways of darkness trod,
Meet face to face, and heart to heart,
  His sin-avenging God?

My Judge and my Creator,
  If I presume to stand
Amid thy pure and holy ones,
  It is at thy command,
To lay before thy mercy's seat
  My sorrows and my fears,
To wail my life and kiss thy feet
  In silence and in tears.

O God! that dreadful moment,
  In sickness and in strife,
When death and hell seem'd watching
  For the last weak pulse of life,
When on the waves of sin and pain
  My drowning soul was toss'd,
Thy hand of mercy saved me then,
  When hope itself was lost.

I hear Thy voice, my Saviour,
  It speaks within my breast,
"Oh, come to me, thou weary one,
  I'll hush thy cares to rest";

Then from the parch'd and burning waste
Of sin, where long I trod,
I come to thee, thou stream of life,
My Saviour and my God!

J. J. Callanan

PARAPHRASE OF ST. THOMAS AQUINAS

With all the pow'rs my poor heart hath
Of humble love and loyal faith,
Thus low, my hidden Life, I bow to Thee
Whom too much love hath bow'd more low for me.
Down, down proud sense! discourses die.
Keep close, my soul's inquiring eye!
Nor touch nor taste must look for more
But each sit still in his own door.

Richard Crashaw

ADORO TE DEVOTE

O Godhead hid, devoutly I adore Thee,
Who truly art within the forms before me;
To Thee my heart I bow with bended knee,
As failing quite in contemplating Thee;
God only on the Cross lay hid from view;
But here lies hid at once the manhood too;
And I, in both professing my belief,
Make the same prayer as the repentant thief.
Thy wounds, as Thomas saw, I do not see,
Yet Thee confess my Lord and God to be.
Make me believe Thee ever more and more,
In Thee my hope, in Thee my love to store.
O Thou Memorial of Our Lord's own dying,
O living Bread to mortals life supplying,
Make Thou my soul henceforth on Thee to live,
Ever a taste of heavenly sweetness give!

St. Thomas Aquinas (translated by Edward Caswall)

CORAM SANCTISSIMO

Beautiful, O Love, Thou art,
Print Thine image on my heart!
Fairer than the rising sun,
Fairer than the dawn begun,
Fairer than the morning star,
Fairer, my Beloved, far
Than all earthly loveliness
Is Thy mystical caress!

Beautiful, O Love, Thy face,
Beautiful, O Love, this quiet place
Where Thy glory dwells content
In the Blessed Sacrament.
Beautiful this mystery
Of a God's humility,
Beautiful Thy smile above
Weary millions seeking love.

Mary Dixon Thayer

I PRAY FOR ONE I LOVE

To You, O Lord, behind the curtained door,
Impelled by faith I come now to implore
For one I love the grace to find You there,
To live no longer of You unaware.

He thinks the darkness light, delays to seek
What You delight to give the lowly meek.
But, since no man more honest You have made,
O let his heart be troubled and afraid.

Beyond the acclamations of the crowd
Let loneliness enclose him like a shroud.
If needful, let betrayal of a friend
Discover to him Godhead in the end.

Without a heritage of faith I'd be
A far less stalwart friend of men than he.

Who follows all the light the darkness gives
Deserves to see the sun by which love lives.

Sister Miriam

AN EVENING VISIT

I come before Thee, Lord, at close of day
  My soul with fears and sad misgivings stirred;
Too tired to pray, I kneel before Thy face
  And lay my burden down without a word.
I gaze in silence on the little door
  That keeps love's Prisoner in thrall,
Nor ask for more; my troubled heart has room
  For naught save this one thought,—"Thou knowest all."

Tired! It seems as if I could not bear
  Another day the cross that is my share,
The hidden cross that frets my spirit more
  Than all life's ceaseless toil and anxious care;
The daily cross that others never see,
  Or, seeing, smile, perchance, that weight so slight
Could make me falter. (Ah, no heart but Thine
  Its weary pain to me can gauge aright!)

Faint-hearted!—for the way seems long and hard,
  And everywhere the cruel thorns are strown,
And it would seem as if Thy chastening love
  Had bid me tread that bitter path alone.
Faithless! The task committed to my charge
  Is marred with imperfections in Thy sight,
And many a fault in infidelity
  Thine eye hath marked, since dawned the morning light.

Discouraged!—yes, for never feeble will
  Was half so frail and full of change as mine;
Yet do I gather strength to try anew
  Beneath the pity of Thy glance divine.
No lesser love could ever understand
  How I could mean so well and do so ill,

Or find the cause of many a humbling fall
 In wayward impulse, not in traitor will.

The pain of perseverance, the fatigue
 Augmented by each toiling step and slow,
Till 'neath a straw's light weight my soul seems crushed,
 All these, dear Lord, Thy Sacred Heart doth know.
Thou art the only friend who, reading deep
 The inner self, from careless eyes concealed,
Dost draw back with lessened love before
 The waywardness and weakness there revealed.

And who save Thee could pardon thus each fault,
 Reading the effort none beside would see,
Bearing as tenderly the thousandth time
 As if Thou ne'er before hadst pardoned me?
Kind hearts and true I sometimes find, to give
 The alms of cheering word and helping hand,
To counsel, to encourage, sympathize,
 But only Thou, dear Christ, dost understand.

I rise to go. I've breathed no word of prayer,
 Yet is my spirit tranquil with the peace
Of Thy sweep pardon, like a mother's kiss
 That soothes our fears and bids our grieving cease.
And courage new is mine, my cross to bear
 As long as Thou dost will, along life's way,
Although I thought, but one short hour ago,
 I could not brook its weight another day.

One parting gift, sweet Jesus, I would ask;
 Not granted heart's desire, surcease from fear,
Nor lifted cross. This only is my plea:
 Give me, dear Lord, the grace to persevere!
Draw me to Thee, though it should meet the scourge
 Of bitter grief to bring me to Thy feet;
And teach me, when life's path is full of pain,
 To find my solace in Thy presence sweet.

Sister Mary Angelita

IMMOLATION

On taut air—bells; lifted, adoring eyes;
and, sinner, seraph, GOD, look upon God.

Honour to Thee and praise!
Love unto Thee and praise!
Honour and love to Thee, O Lord, and praise.

Christ, star-told in the east,
Christ, lover of "these least"
Christ of the marriage-feast
in this White Host.

Christ by the kings adored,
Christ come to bring the sword,
Christ the Incarnate Word
in this White Host.

Christ of the uncast stone,
Christ in the Garden prone,
Christ agonized, alone
in this White Host.

Christ with ensanguined cheek,
Christ from the scourging weak,
Christ with his mockers meek
in this White Host.

Christ of the supper room,
Christ of the empty tomb,
Christ of the Day of Doom
in this White Host.

Who was, before the Sun,
Who lived, ere Life begun,
Who shall, when Time be done,
in this White Host.

Who dreamed this realm of earth,
Who called the seas to birth,

Who made the stars for mirth,
in this White Host.

Who Glory is and Light,
Who Majesty and Might,
Who fullness of Delight,
in this White Host.

Who dread Divinity,
Who One in Trinity,
Who is Infinity,
in this White Host.

Jesu, with Magdalen I join my plea,
with him who craved remembrance
from the tree,
with drowning Peter: "Lord deliver me"
by this White Host.

Robert Farren

BEFORE AND AFTER HOLY COMMUNION

"THIS IS THE DAY WHICH THE LORD HATH MADE"

This is the day which the Lord hath made: let us be glad and rejoice therein. . . .
Thou art my God, and I will praise thee: thou art my God, and I will exalt thee.
I will praise thee, because thou hast heard me, and art become my salvation.
O praise ye the Lord, for he is good: for his mercy endureth for ever.

Psalm 117:24, 28–9

OUR DAILY BREAD

Give us our daily Bread,
O God, the bread of strength!
For we have learnt to know
How weak we are at length.
As children we are weak,
As children must be fed;—
Give us Thy Grace, O Lord,
To be our daily Bread.

Give us our daily Bread:—
The bitter bread of grief.
We sought earth's poisoned feasts
For pleasure and relief;
We sought her deadly fruits,
But now, O God, instead,
We ask thy healing grief
To be our daily Bread.

Give us our daily Bread
To cheer our fainting soul;
The feast of comfort, Lord,
And peace, to make us whole:
For we are sick of tears,
The useless tears we shed;—
Now give us comfort, Lord,
To be our daily Bread.

Give us our daily Bread,
The Bread of Angels, Lord,
For us, so many times,
Broken, betrayed, adored:
His Body and His Blood;—
The feast that Jesus spread:
Give Him—our life, our all—
To be our daily Bread!

Adelaide Anne Procter

HOLY COMMUNION

Disguised He stands without in the street;
Far come is He on heavy feet.
O heart of mine, open thy gate;
For darkness falls, and it is late!

Lord of the heaven's fairest height,
Homeless in the traveler's night,
Begging my hearth, my board, my cup,
That I, not He, may richly sup.

O soul of mine, the board begin,
And let this wondrous Beggar in!

Speer Strahan

JESUS, THOU JOY OF LOVING HEARTS

Jesus, thou joy of loving hearts,
  Thou Fount of life, thou Light of men,
From the best bliss that earth imparts,
  We turn unfilled to thee again.

Thy truth unchanged hath ever stood;
  Thou savest those who on Thee call;
To them that seek Thee, Thou art good,
  To them that find Thee, all in all.

We taste Thee, O Thou living Bread,
  And long to feast upon Thee still;
We drink of Thee the Fountain-head,
  And thirst, our souls from Thee to fill.

Our restless spirits yearn for Thee,
  Where'er our changeful lot is cast;
Glad, when Thy gracious smile we see,
  Blest, when our faith can hold Thee fast.

O Jesus, ever with us stay;
  Make all our moments calm and bright;

Chase the dark night of sin away;
  Shed o'er the world thy holy light.

St. Bernard of Clairvaux

"LORD, TO THINE ALTAR LET ME GO"

Lord, to Thine altar let me go,
The child of weariness and woe,
  My home to find;
From sin and sense and self set free,
Absorbed alone in love of Thee,
Able to leave in liberty
  This world behind.

Jesus, be Thou my heavenly Food,
Sweet source divine of every good,
  Center of rest;
One with Thy heart let me be found,
Prostrate upon that holy ground,
Where grace and peace and life abound
  Drawn from Thy breast.

Madeline Bridges

BEFORE COMMUNION

O Saviour, who lightest the sun's blessed ray,
Remit my offenses, this day and alway,
Above my deserving, or all I could pay;
Then with joy I receive my Redeemer today.

Anonymous (translated from the Gaelic by Eleanor Hull)

THE UNKNOWN GOD

One of the crowd went up,
And knelt before the Paten and the Cup,

Received the Lord, returned in peace, and prayed
Close to my side. Then in my heart I said:

"O Christ in this man's life—
This stranger who is Thine—in all his strife,
All his felicity, his good and ill,
In the assaulted stronghold of his will,

"I do confess Thee here,
Alive within this life; I know Thee near
Within this lonely conscience, closed away
Within this brother solitary day.

"Christ in his unknown heart,
His intellect unknown—this love, this art,
This battle and this peace, this destiny
That I shall never know—look upon me!

"Christ in his numbered breath,
Christ in his beating heart and in his death,
Christ in his mystery! From that secret place
And from that separate dwelling, give me grace!"

Alice Meynell

THANKSGIVING AFTER COMMUNION

Jesus, gentlest Saviour!
  God of might and power!
Thou Thyself are dwelling
  In us at this hour.

Nature cannot hold Thee,
  Heaven is all too strait
For Thine endless glory,
  And Thy royal state.

Out beyond the shining
  Of the furthest star,

Thou art ever stretching
  Infinitely far.

Yet hearts of children
  Hold what worlds cannot,
And the God of wonders
  Loves the lowly spot.

As men to their gardens
  Go to seek sweet flowers,
In our hearts dear Jesus
  Seeks them at all hours.

Jesus, gentlest Saviour!
  Thou art in us now;
Fill us full of goodness,
  Till our hearts o'erflow.

Pray the prayer within us
  That to heaven shall rise;
Sing the song that angels
  Sing above the skies.

Multiply our graces,
  Chiefly love and fear,
And, dear Lord! the chiefest—
  Grace to persevere.

Oh, how can we thank Thee
  For a gift like this,
Gift that truly maketh
  Heaven's eternal bliss?

Ah! when wilt Thou always
Make our hearts Thy home?
We must wait for heaven,—
  Then the day will come.

Now at least we'll keep Thee
  All the time we may;

But Thy grace and blessing
We will keep alway.

When our hearts Thou leavest,
Worthless though they be,
Give them to Thy Mother
To be kept for Thee.

Frederick W. Faber

ASPIRATION

Preserve, my Jesus, oh preserve
My soul to everlasting life.
O may this blest communion serve
To aid my soul in passion's strife:
Oh, may Thy Body, may Thy Blood,
Be to my soul a saving food,
To fill it still with life and grace,
And every sinful stain efface.

J. Beste

POST-COMMUNION

Lord, when to Thine embrace I run,
Gathered like waters to the Sun,
Shape me to such celestial mirth
As may go back and glad the earth.
Let Thy rays compass me, and crowd
Into the semblance of a cloud
Mine idle and dispersèd powers;
That I, the casket of Thy showers,
May, for my closeness, coloured be
(How'er so faintly) like to Thee;

And when Thou loosest me to go
Diffused into Thy world below
May I, till drip of words shall cease,
Sing of Refreshment, Light and Peace;

And, poured into the Time's abyss,
Revive one blossom for Thy bliss.

Helen Parry Eden

AFTER COMMUNION

I am my love's, and He is mine;
In me He dwells; in Him I live;
What greater gifts could love combine?
What greater could e'en heaven give?
O sacred banquet, heavenly feast!
O overflowing source of grace!
Where God the food, and man the guest,
Meet and unite in sweet embrace!

William Young

HOLY COMMUNION IN A HOSPITAL

All of my life I have come to You, walking erect, hands clasped, head a little bowed;
Finding my way to You through the Sunday, the everyday crowd;
Kneeling to wait till You came to me in Your inexplicable way,
Leaving me shaken with love and with less than nothing to say;
Always I came to You so; always until today.

Today You will come to me here in this room half-lighted, curtains a little drawn.
Never before have You sought me so, brought me Yourself at dawn.
Now You are helplessly here more than I, to feed me, to comfort, to bless;
Infinite, patient to bear with me pain's relentless caress;
Clothing me with Yourself, in the vesture of helplessness.

Sister M. Madeleva

COMMUNION

Mother Mary, thee I see
Bringing Him, thy Babe, to me,

Thou dost say, with trusting smile:
"Hold him, dear, a little while."
Mother Mary, pity me,
For He struggles to be free!
My heart, my arms—He finds defiled:
I am unworthy of thy Child.
Mary, Mother, charity!
Bring thy Baby back to me!

Caroline Giltinan

MORNING PRAYER-POEMS

"GIVE EAR, O LORD, TO MY WORD"

Give ear, O Lord, to my word, understand my cry.
Hearken to the voice of my prayer, O my King and my God.
For to thee will I pray: O Lord, in the morning thou shalt hear my voice.
In the morning I will stand before thee, and will see: because thou art not a God that willest iniquity.

Psalm 5:2–5

MORNING HYMN

Lo, fainter now lie spread the shades of night,
And upward spread the trembling gleams of morn;
Suppliant we bend before the Lord of Light,
And pray at early dawn,

That his sweet charity may all our sin
Forgive, and make our miseries to cease;
May grant us health, grant us the gift divine
Of everlasting peace.

Father Supreme, this grace on us confer;
And Thou, O Son, by an eternal birth!
With Thee coequal spirit comforter!
Whose glory fills the earth.

Pope St. Gregory the Great (translated by Edward Caswall)

MORNING
From St. Gregory Nazianzen

I rise and raise my clasped hands to Thee!
Henceforth, the darkness has no part of me,
Thy sacrifice this day,
Abiding firm, and with a freeman's might
Stemming the waves of passion in the fight;—
Ah, should I from Thee stray,
My hoary head, Thy table where I bow,
Will be my shame, which are mine honours now.
Thus I set out—Lord! lead men on the way!

John Henry Newman

BLESSED BE THE HOLY WILL OF GOD
A Morning Prayer

The will of God be done by us.
The law of God be kept by us,
Our evil will controlled by us,

Our tongue in check be held by us,
Repentance timely made by us,
Christ's passion understood by us,
Each sinful crime be shunned by us,
Much on the *End* be mused by us,
And Death be blessed found by us,
With Angels' music heard by us,
And God's high praise sung to us,
For ever and for aye.

Anonymous (translated from the Gaelic by Douglas Hyde)

MORNING HYMN

What's this morn's bright eye to me,
If I see not Thine and Thee,
Fairer JESU; in whose face
All my Heaven is spread!—Alas,
Still I grovel in dead night,
Whilst I want Thy living light;
Dreaming with wide open eyes
Fond fantastic vanities.

Shine, my only Day-Star, shine:
So mine eyes shall wake by Thine;
So the dreams I grope in now
To clear visions all shall grow;
So my day shall measured be
By Thy Grace's clarity;
So shall I discern the path
Thy sweet law prescribed hath;
For Thy ways cannot be shown
By any light but by Thine own.

Joseph Beaumont

EVENING PRAYER-POEMS

"THE HEAVENS SHEW FORTH THE GLORY OF GOD"

The heavens shew forth the glory of God, and the firmament declareth the work of his hands.

Psalm 18:2

HYMN FOR THE LIGHTING OF THE LAMPS

Hail, gladdening Light, of his pure glory poured
  Who is the Immortal Father, heavenly blest,
Holiest of Holies, Jesus Christ, Our Lord.
  Now we are come to the sun's hour of rest,
The lights of evening round us shine,
We hymn the Father, Son and Holy Spirit divine.
Worthiest art Thou at all times to be sung
With undefilèd tongue,
Son of our God, giver of life alone.
Therefore in all the world, Thy glories, Lord, they own.

Attributed to St. Athenogenes, a Martyr of the Second Century
(translated by John Keble)

AVE MARIA

Fading, still fading, the last beam is shining,
  Ave Maria! day is declining;
Safety and innocence fly with the light,
Temptation and danger walk forth in the night;
From the fall of the shade, till the matin shall chime,
Shield us from danger, and save us from crime.

Thomas O. Davis

EVENING
From St. Gregory Nazianzen

O Holiest Truth! how have I lied to Thee!
  I vow'd this day Thy festival should be:
    But I am dim ere night.
Surely I made my prayer, and did deem
That I could keep in me Thy morning beam,
      Immaculate and bright;
But my foot slipp'd; and as I lay, he came,
My gloomy foe, and robb'd me of heaven's flame.
Help Thou my darkness, Lord, till I am light.

John Henry Newman

"THE SHADOWS OF THE EVENING HOURS"

The shadows of the evening hours
  Fall from the darkening sky;
Upon the fragrance of the flowers
  The dews of evening lie.

Before Thy throne, O Lord of heaven,
  We kneel at close of day;
Look on Thy children from on high,
  And hear us while we pray.

The sorrows of Thy servants, Lord,
  Oh, do not Thou despise,
But let the incense of our prayers
  Before Thy mercy rise.

The brightness of the coming night
  Upon the darkness rolls;
With hopes of future glory chase
  The shadows on our souls.

Slowly the rays of daylight fade:
  So fade within our heart
The hopes in earthly love and joy,
  That one by one depart.

Slowly the bright stars, one by one,
  Within the heavens shine;
Give us, O Lord, fresh hopes from heaven,
  And trust in things divine.

Let peace, O Lord, Thy peace, O God,
  Upon our souls descend;
From midnight fears, and perils, Thou
  Our trembling hearts defend.

Give us a respite from our toil;
  Calm and subdue our woes;

Through the long day we labor, Lord,
Oh, give us now repose.

Adelaide Anne Procter

A NIGHT PRAYER

May the will of God be done by us,
May the death of the saints be won by us,
And the lights of the kingdom begun in us;
May Jesus the Child be beside my bed,
May the Lamb of mercy uplift my head,
May the Virgin her heavenly brightness shed,
And Michael be steward of my soul!

Anonymous (translated from the Gaelic by Eleanor Hull)

"MOTHER OF GOD!"

Mother of God! as evening falls,
Upon the silent sea,
And shadows veil the mountain walls
We lift our souls to thee!
From lurking perils of the night,
The desert's hidden harms,
From plagues that waste, from blows that smite,
Defend thy men-at-arms.

Mother of God! thy starry smile
Still bless us from above!
Keep pure our souls from passion's guile,
Our hearts from earthly love!
Still save each soul from guilt apart
As stainless as each sword;
And guard undimmed in every heart
The image of our Lord!

John Hay

LUX IN TENEBRIS

At night when things will stalk abroad,
  What veilèd shapes and eyes of dread!
With phantoms in a lonely road
  And visions of the dead.

The kindly room when day is here,
  At night takes ghostly terrors on;
And every shadow has its fear,
  And every wind its moan.

Lord Jesus, Day-Star of the world,
  Rise, Thou, and bid this dark depart,
And all the east, a rose uncurled,
  Grow golden at the heart!

Lord, in the watches of the night,
  Keep Thou my soul! a trembling thing
As any moth that in daylight
  Will spread a rainbow wing.

Katharine Tynan Hinkson

CONFIDED

Another lamb, O Lord of God, behold,
  Within this quiet fold,
  Among Thy Father's sheep.
  I lay to sleep!
A heart that never for a night did rest
  Beyond its mother's breast.
  Lord keep it close to Thee,
Lest waking it should bleat and pine for me!

John Banister Tabb

GOOD NIGHT!

Good night, dear Lord! and now
  Let them that loved to keep

Thy little bed in Bethlehem,
  Be near me while I sleep;
For I—more helpless, Lord—of them
  Have greater need than Thou.

John Banister Tabb

I REST WITH THEE, O JESUS

I rest with Thee, O Jesus,
  And do Thou rest with me.
The oil of Christ on my poor soul,
The creed of the Twelve to make me whole,
  Above my head I see.
O Father, who created me,
O Son, who purchased me,
O Spirit Blest, who blesseth me,
  Rest ye with me.

Anonymous (translated from the Gaelic by Eleanor Hull)

THANKSGIVING AND GRATITUDE

"COME LET US PRAISE THE LORD WITH JOY"

Come let us praise the Lord with joy: let us joyfully sing to God our saviour.
Let us come before his presence with thanksgiving; and make a joyful noise to him with psalms.
For the Lord is a great God, and a great King above all gods.

Psalm 94:1–3

THANKSGIVING

The roar of the world is my ears.
  Thank God for the roar of the world!
Thank God for the mighty tide of fears
  Against me always hurled!

Thank God for the bitter and ceaseless strife,
  And the sting of His chastening rod!
Thank God for the stress and pain of life,
  And, oh, thank God for God!

Francis Thompson

FOR TRINITY SUNDAY

O God, by Whose command is swayed
This ordered world which Thou hast made;
Parent of heavenly clemency,
In nature One, in persons Three;
Assist us while our minds we raise,
Inflamed with Thy immortal praise;
That with our sober thoughts, we may
Forever our thanksgiving pay.

Roman Breviary

A GRATEFUL HEART

Thou hast given so much to me,
Give one thing more—a grateful heart;
Not thankful when it pleaseth me,
As if Thy blessings had spare days;
But such a heart, whose pulse may be
Thy praise.

George Herbert

THANKS GIVEN

There is so much to thank Thee for,
  Thy favors are so great,

My heart seems breaking, dear my Lord,
Beneath this precious weight.

I thank Thee then for these my eyes,
My happy eyes that see
The beauty in the silver rain,
The May mist on the sea.

I thank Thee, Lord, that I can hear
With breathless joy, a song,
And draw it to my very heart
And hold it all day long.

I thank thee, Lord, that I can walk
Beneath the skies at night,
Through scented streets where spring has passed
With robes of starlit white.

I thank Thee, O Thou Crucified,
That I have known the pain
Of giving what I longed to keep,
That their's might be the gain.

I thank Thee, Lord, that I have loved,
With all my poor heart's best,
And never once the trust betrayed
Each dear love strangely blest.

I thank Thee, Lord, oh most of all,
For this sweet sense of Thee,
This blessed sense that fills me through,
With singing ecstasy.

Eleanor M. Leary

HIS HIC ALIENIGENA

A stranger in Thy Church am I; my days
Dawned otherwhere; until my life is spent
I shall not speak Thy language, learn Thy ways,

Or draw one breath without bewilderment.
Yet would I kneel before Thee with that man
Of Thy ten lepers cured the only one
Who hastened back—Thy poor Samaritan—
To thank and bless Thee when the rest were gone.

Helen Parry Eden

THE UNDISCOVERED COUNTRY

Lord, for the erring thought
Not until evil wrought:
Lord, for the wicked will
Betrayed and baffled still:
For the heart from itself kept,
Our thanksgiving accept.
For the ignorant hopes that were
Broken to our blind prayer:
For pain, death, sorrow sent
Unto our chastisement:
For all loss of seeming good,
Quicken our gratitude.

William Dean Howells

GRACE FOR A SPRING MORNING

O God, dear Architect of this bright day,
Thanks for the antique courtesy of spring,
Unlocking winter's grip along the land,
Releasing every creature from his grief.
For light streams back now Thy relenting sun
Awaken us like an unhoped-for kiss,
And common earth is carpeted with grace.

Now have the spacious precincts of the sun
Become again our Father's shining house,
Columned with cedar, decked for our delight
In fragrant petals and enameled wings.

Forgive Thy churlish guests this April day
And grant our deepening praises, spring by spring,
May yet reclaim us as Thy sons. Amen.

Frances Stoakley Lankford

THANKS

My God, I think Thee who hast made
The Earth so bright;
So full of splendor and of joy,
Beauty and light;
So many glorious things are here,
Noble and right!

I thank Thee, too, that Thou hast made
Joy to abound;
So many good thoughts and deeds
Circling us round,
That in the darkest spot of Earth
Some love is found.

I thank Thee *more* that all our joy
Is touched with pain;
That shadows fall on brightest hours;
That thorns remain;
So that Earth's bliss may be our guide,
And not our chain.

For Thou Who knowest, Lord, how soon
Our weak heart clings,
Hast given us joys, tender and true,
Yet all with wings,
So that we see, gleaming on high,
Diviner things!
I thank Thee Lord, that Thou hast kept
The best in store;
We have enough, yet not too much
To long for more:

A yearning for a deeper peace,
Not known before.

I thank Thee, Lord, that here our souls,
Though amply blest,
Can never find, although they seek,
A perfect rest,—
Nor ever shall, until they lean
On Jesus' breast!

Adelaide Anne Procter

IN HUMBLENESS

Lord Jesus, I have ofttimes sued
To You, but now in gratitude
I thank You for my happy days
Of golden hours and pleasant ways.

I thank You for my life of ease
Under blue skies by tranquil seas,
For sun and stars that shine above
The common things of life and love.

I thank You that You gave to me
No fierce protracted agony
Wherein the body clouds the soul
In its long striving for the goal.

I thank You that when sorrow came
You taught me how to cry Your name
And in that moment You, my Guide,
Showed me Your Hands, Your Wounded Side.

I thank You that You bade me call
Your Mother mine, and knowing all
My need, You willed my prayer should be,
Mother of Jesus, pray for me.

I thank You that You set me in
Ways so removed from lure of sin,
Nor willed temptation should assail
One prone, alas, to faint and fail.

I thank You too that day by day
You drew me closer to You to pray,
Enfolded to Your Sacred Heart
In many a mystic hour apart.

You knew my little strength, and made
Life easy for me; grace and aid
Were never lacking . . . Lord, I see
How tender You have been to me.

Isabel C. Clarke

HOLY INFANT OF GOOD HEALTH

You are making it easy for us, Niño
Crossing out the past
And starting us out from that nothingness
Only on which,
    Your Holy Spirit can build . . .

Easy,
For as over the nocolor abyss
HE hovered
And created this world:
Our souls HE builds into homes
Where You, Niño, and Your Father
And that same Spirit can live.

Howard Hart

THE THANKSGIVING OF THE CHASTENED

For the pain, as well as the pleasure,
  For the woe, as well as the weal;

For the loss of the dearest treasure,
  And the wound no balm can heal;
For the bloom, and the blight that kill'd it,
  Scant sun, and the shadow broad—
Since Thy love hath, in wisdom, willed it—
  We thank Thee, Lord, our God!

For the tears that the heart-strings rusted,
  For the gold half-dimm'd with dross;
For the change in the friend long trusted,
  For the scourge, the thorn, and the cross;
Because they have shown us clearer
  The path Thy feet once trod;
Have drawn us nearer and nearer
  To Thee—we thank Thee, God!

For the sad mistake that was blameless
  For the sinless dark disgrace,
For the sorrow, hidden and nameless,
  That won us Thy close embrace!
For the dead, as well as the living,
  For the stricken under the rod—
With a joy, not of earth's thanksgiving,
  We thank Thee, Lord, our God!

Eleanor C. Donnelly

A GRACE

Great Giver of the open hand,
We stand to thank Thee for our meat,
A hundred praises, Christ, 'tis meet,
For all we drink, for all we eat.

Anonymous

FOR HAVING THEE

I thank Thee, Lord, for this good life,
For Water, Oil, Wine, Wafer, Wife,

For time to do a Penance in
And grace to half forget the sin,
For father's smile and mother's tears
And sister's salutary fears,
For friendships firm and friendships fleeting,
For adieus and happy meeting,
For laughter running like a boy,
For prick of pain foretelling joy,
For leaps the heart makes at the sense
Of sacramental innocence,
For having Thee to thank and praise,
Adore and hope for all our days.

Francis X. Connolly

DEDICATION

"THE LINES ARE FALLEN UNTO ME IN GOODLY PLACES"

The lines are fallen unto me in goodly places: for my inheritance is goodly to me.
I will bless the Lord, who hath given me understanding: moreover my reins also have corrected me even till night.
I set the Lord always in my sight: for he is at my right hand, that I be not moved.
Therefore my heart hath been glad, and my tongue hath rejoiced: moreover my flesh also shall rest in hope.

Psalm 15:6–9

BEFORE PERPETUAL VOWS

Lord, give this to me:
A perilous uncertainty.
I have desired
To desire.
Strike, if so it please Thee,
Strike, Thou, the fire,
Or if Thou wouldst, leave me
To desire.
For my security
I ask this aching need of Thee.

So shall I take the thin-webbed mail
Of the veil
As a helmet of salvation unto Life.

Sister Mary Maura

PROCESS

The seed, Lord, falls on stony ground
Which sun and rain can never bless—
Until the soil is broken found—
With harvest fruitfulness.

Plow then the rock, and plow again,
That so some blade of good may start,
After the searching share of pain
Has cut furrow through my heart.

Charles L. O'Donnell

CONSECRATION

How great the tale, that there should be,
In God's Son's heart, a place for me!
That on a sinner's lips like mine,
The cross of Jesus Christ should shine!

Christ Jesus bend me to Thy will,
My feet to urge, my griefs to still;
That even my flesh and blood may be
A temple sanctified to Thee.

No rest, no calm, my soul may win,
Because my body craves to sin;
Till Thou, dear Lord, Thyself impart
Peace to my head, light to my heart.

May consecration come from far,
Soft shining like the evening star!
My toilsome path makes plain to me,
Until I come to rest in Thee.

Murdock O'Daly (translated by Eleanor Hull)

FOR AN ORDINAND

God give His flame of Love
To light the fires of your heart:
The puring Pentecostal Flame
To every priestly grace impart.

God give the Flame of knowledge clear
To light the fibres of your brain,
And send sure words of wisdom out
Your priestly lips . . . a glad refrain.

God give the Flame of courage bright
The Flame of consolation for
Yourself and those who seek your care:
God give you these a hundred fold and more.

William Noé Field

PSALM FOR ORDERS

Make of me what Thou wouldst, My God:
A plough, a sword, an eagle black against the sky:

A book, a torch, a battle flag to fly:
  A root, a tree, a square-set cornerstone:
A temple of my very flesh and bone.

Beat me out upon Thy forge,
  Fan the puring flames with Love Divine:
Test me hard against Thy Hand
  With all devices that are Thine.

Only use me, Lord, a poor, mis-shapen thing . . .
  Then may I wander not
To serve another King.

William Noé Field

UNEARTH
(Her daughter takes the veil)

Gardener of Eden and Gethsemane,
Gently unearth this rosebush that has grown
In the sunken garden of my heart, and be
Gentle to her who yields it yet unblown.
Gardener of Eden, where this tender stem
Henceforth will be the strength of other fingers,
And these leaves brush another's garment hem—
You will not care if round the root there lingers
Something of native soil to swell the bud
Till that root sinks in You as once in me . . .
Unearth the rosebush of my flesh and blood,
Gardener of Eden—and Gethsemane!

Alfred Barrett

TO THE HOLY GHOST

O boundless ocean of the Holy Ghost,
  Receive me as Thy shell
That I may be an echo of Thy song
  In every place I dwell.

Let him who stops to listen at my heart
Be magnetized by Sea
And follow, follow inward and be lost
And cast himself in Thee.

Jessica Powers

PATRON OF THE CHURCH

Saint Joseph, whom the Lord hath willed
To keep His Church and guard His Host,
Be patron of the church I build
As dwelling for the Holy Ghost.

Encircle it with silences,
The rampart of a house of prayer,
And set a lamp for emphasis
Upon a sacred Presence there.

This is the Spirit's residence
And carries heaven by His grace.
Instruct me in the reverence
Becoming to a holy place.

O more than humble carpenter,
O thou who are eternally
God's architect and almoner,
Build thou thyself this church in me.

I would it were of marble hewn,
The pure word *white* defined in stone,
Set me on a page of southern noon,
And none were there save God alone,

The Spirit singing, all unheard,
The song of His Divinity,
Loving the Father and the Word
In surges of infinity.

I pray thee in the name of her
Who was God's only undefiled,

The Spirit's bride and worshipper
Who in His shadow bore her Child,

Construct and consecrate in love
This house where bride and spirit meet
And be the Lord and patron of
This chapel of the Paraclete.

Jessica Powers

CONSECRATION

Just as I am, Thine own to be,
Friend of the young, who lovest me,
To consecrate myself to Thee,
O Jesus Christ, I come.

In the glad morning of my day,
My life I give, my vows to pay,
With no reserve and no delay,
With all my heart I come.

I would live ever in the light,
I would work ever for the right,
I would serve Thee with all my might;
Therefore, to Thee, I come.

Just as I am, young, strong and free,
To be the best that I can be
For truth, and righteousness and Thee,
Lord of my life, I come.

Marianne Hearn

VOCATION

Dear Lord,
I saw the beauty of the earth,
The trees, the flowers,
All: I saw the children's mirth,

I felt the gentle breeze.
  I heard the birds' sweet call,
I loved it all:
  And yet, I longed for more—
Something to fill the void
  Within my soul,
Something whole,
Something—I knew not what,
Something that contained each joy:
  Each, all, and yet
Where'er I turned I found alloy.
  Until—Ah! sweet and wonderful
I heard Thy voice:
  That I must come to Thee,
Must rest at last in Thee.
  My love
I come, my heart is Thine alone,
  Complete Thy love, and take
  me for Thine own.

Anonymous

"TEACH ME, O GOD"

Teach me, O God, to do without the things
  That men most seek and love, as wealth and fame,
  And wife and children, and an empty name,
And all to which the heart most fondly clings;

That I may find the source whence pure joy springs,
  And make Thy love of all life sole aim,
  With not a thought or wish to thwart Thy claim
To my poor heart, which to Thee nothing brings.

John Lancaster Spalding

SEND ME

Use me, God, in Thy great harvest field,
Which stretcheth far and wide like a wide sea;

The gatherers are so few; I fear the precious yield
Will suffer loss. Oh, find a place for me!
A place where best the strength I have will tell:
It may be one the older toilers shun;
Be it a wide or narrow place, 'tis well
So that the work it holds be only done.

Christina Rossetti

"TAKE MY LIFE"

Take my life, and let it be
Consecrated, Lord, to Thee.
Take my moments and my days;
Let them flow in ceaseless praise.
Take my hands, and let them move
At the impulse of Thy love.
Take my feet and let them be
Swift and beautiful for Thee.

Take my voice, and let me sing,
Always, only, for my King.
Take my lips, and let them be
Filled with messages from Thee.
Take my silver and my gold;
Not a mite would I withhold.
Take my intellect, and use
Every power as Thou shalt choose.

Take my will, and make it Thine;
It shall be no longer mine.
Take my heart, it is Thine own;
It shall be Thy royal throne.
Take my love; my Lord, I pour
At Thy feet its treasure-store.
Take myself, and I will be
Ever, only, all for Thee.

Frances Ridley Havergal

CHANT OF DEPARTURE
A Missionary's Prayer

Woman who walked home on the arm of John
Another way from that your Son had gone,
Woman who walked
And talked,
Unwavering, of what must yet be done—
Woman, behold your son!

Behold
Him who in boyhood haunts will not grow old;
Who goes predestined to an alien grave
In clay or sand or wave—
Yet sails enamored of one hope: to see,
As John from his dawn-lit faces on the shore
At Shantung or the coast of Travancore.

Woman who walked home on the arm of John,
When on
Some night of tears I hear the palm trees toss,
Stand by my side beneath the Southern Cross.

Alfred Barrett

FOR PROTECTION AND PEACE

"IN THEE, O LORD, HAVE I HOPED"

In thee, O Lord, have I hoped, let me never be confounded: deliver me in thy justice.
Bow down thy ear to me: make haste to deliver me.
Be thou unto me a God, a protector, and a house of refuge, to save me.
For thou art my strength and my refuge; and for thy name's sake thou wilt lead me, and nourish me. . . .
Into thy hands I commend my spirit: thou hast redeemed me, O Lord, the God of truth.

Psalm 30:1–4, 6

CONSOLATION

When I sink down in gloom or fear,
  Hope blighted or delay'd,
Thy whisper, Lord, my heart shall cheer,
  " 'Tis I, be not afraid!"

Or, startled at some sudden blow,
  If fretful thoughts I feel,
"Fear not, it is but I!" shall flow,
  As balm my wound to heal.

John Henry Newman

FOR ALL WHO NEED

For all who watch tonight—by land or sea or air—
O Father, may they know that Thou art with them there.

For all who weep tonight, the hearts that cannot rest,
Reveal Thy love, that wondrous love which gave for us Thy best.

For all who wake tonight, love's tender watch to keep,
Watcher Divine, Thyself draw nigh, Thou who dost never sleep.

For all who fear tonight, whate'er the dread may be,
We ask for them the perfect peace of hearts that rest in Thee.

Our own beloved tonight, O Father, keep, and where
Our love and succor cannot reach, now bless them through our prayer.

And all who pray tonight, Thy wrestling hosts, O Lord,
Make weakness strong, let them prevail according to Thy word.

Anonymous

"DEAR JESUS, SAVIOR OF THE WORLD"

Dear Jesus, Savior of the world,
  Our Savior be today;

Protect our hearts in darkness hurled,
And guide us in Thy way.

Pope St. Gregory the Great (translated by D. Donahoe)

GOD KEEP YOU

God keep you, dearest, all this lonely night:
The winds are still,
The moon drops down behind the western hill;
God keep you safely, dearest, till the light.

God keep you then when slumber melts away,
And care and strife
Take up new arms to fret our waking life,
God keep you through the battle of the day.

God keep you. Nay, beloved soul, how vain,
How poor is prayer!
I can but say again, and yet again,
God keep you every time and everywhere.

Madeline Bridges

TO THE BLESSED VIRGIN

Hail to the Queen who reigns above,
Mother of clemency and love,
Hail, thou, our hope, life, sweetness; we
Eve's banished children cry to Thee.

We from this wretched vale of tears
Send sighs and groans unto thy ears;
O, then, sweet Advocate, bestow
A pitying look on us below.

After this our exile, let us see
Our blessed Jesus, born of thee.

O merciful, O pious Maid,
O gracious Mary, lend thine aid.

Roman Breviary

ORA PRO ME

Ave Maria! bright and pure,
   Hear, O hear me when I pray!
Pains and pleasures try the pilgrim
   On his long and weary way;
Fears and perils are around me,—
   Ora pro me.

Mary, see my heart is burdened,
   Take, O take the weight away,
O help me that I may not murmur
   If it is a cross you lay
On my weak and trembling heart,—but
   Ora pro me.

Mary, Mary, Queen of Heaven,
   Teach, oh teach me to obey:
Lead me on, though fierce temptations
   Stand to meet me in the way;
When I fail and faint, my mother,
   Ora pro me.

Then shall I, if thou, O Mother,
   Art my strong support and stay—
Fear nor feel the threefold danger
   Standing forth in dread array;
Now and ever shield and guard me,
   Ora pro me.

When my eyes are slowly closing,
   And I fade from earth away,
And when Death, the stern destroyer,
   Claims my body, as his prey,—

Claim my soul, and then, sweet Mary,
Ora pro me.

Adelaide Anne Procter

"MOTHER OF GRACE, O MARY BLEST"

Mother of grace, O Mary blest,
To thee, sweet fount of love, we fly:
Shield us through life, and take us hence
To thy dear bosom when we die.

Roman Breviary (translated by Edward Caswall)

AVE MARIA STELLA

Star of ocean fairest,
Mother, God who barest,
Virgin thou immortal
Heaven's blissful portal.

Ave thou receivest,
Gabriel's word believest,
Change to peace and gladness
Eva's name of sadness.

Loose the bonds of terror,
Lighten blinded error,
All our ills repressing,
Pray for every blessing.

Mother's care displaying
Offer him thy praying
Who, when born our Brother
Chose thee for his Mother.

Virgin all-excelling,
Gentle past our telling,
Pardoned sinners render
Gentle, chaste, and tender.

In pure paths direct us,
On our way protect us,
Till, on Jesus gazing,
We shall join thy praising.

Father, Son eternal,
Holy Ghost supernal,
With one praise we bless thee,
Three in One confess thee.

Anonymous

HYMN TO THE VIRGIN

Ave Maria! Maiden mild!
Listen to a maiden's prayer:
Thou canst hear though from the wild,
Thou canst save amid despair.
Safe may we sleep beneath thy care,
Though banished, outcast, and reviled.
Maiden! hear a maiden's prayer;
Mother, hear a suppliant child!
Ave Maria!

Ave Maria! undefiled!
The flinty couch we now must share,
Shall seem with down of eider piled,
If thy protection hover there.
The murky cavern's heavy air
Shall breathe of balm if thou hast smiled;
Then, Maiden, hear a maiden's prayer,
Mother, list a suppliant child!
Ave Maria!

Ave Maria! stainless styled!
Foul demons of the earth and air,
From this their wonted haunt exiled,
Shall flee before thy presence fair.
We bow us to our lot of care,
Beneath thy guidance reconciled;

Hear for a maid a maiden's prayer!
   And for a father hear his child!
      Ave Maria!

Sir Walter Scott

STELLA MATUTINA

Earth and skies the dawn is waking,
   Sunlight bids the shadows flee,
Loving hearts, both glad and aching,
   Turn, O Mother, up to thee!

Thro' the long night just departed,
   Thou hast watched our curtained sleep,
With a care so tender-hearted,
   And a love so deep and true.

Thou hast calmed our restless dreaming,
   While the shadows round us lay:
Now the morning's rays are beaming,
   Wilt thou, Mother, near us stay?

All life's toil and care before us,
   Slipp'ry paths and heights to scale,
If some safeguard be not o'er us,
   What will all our strength avail?

Leave us not, O helpful Mother!
   Hold the hand and guide the feet,
Next to God, there is no other
   Who can shield us from deceit.

Clinging close to thee in weakness,
   We may venture forth again.
In the eve, O Maid of meekness!
   Lead us back unspotted then.

Eleanor C. Donnelly

MEMORARE

Remember, holy Mary,
'Twas never heard or known
That anyone who sought thee
And made to thee his moan—
That anyone who hastened
For shelter to thy care
Was ever yet abandoned
And left to his despair.

Attributed to St. Bernard of Clairvaux
(translated by Matthew Russell)

FOR PEACE

Lord, make me an instrument of Thy peace.
Where there is hate, may I bring love;
Where offense, may I bring pardon;
May I bring union in place of discord;
Truth, replacing error;
Faith, where once there was doubt;
Hope, for despair;
Light, where was darkness;
Joy to replace sadness.
Make me not to so crave to be loved as to love.
Help me to learn that in giving I may receive;
In forgetting self, I may find life eternal.

St. Francis of Assisi

THE PEACE OF GOD

We ask for Peace, O Lord!
Thy children ask for Peace;
Not what the world calls rest,
That toil and care should cease,
That through bright sunny hours
Calm life should fleet away,

And tranquil night should fade
  In smiling day;—
It is not for such Peace that we would pray.

We ask for Peace, O Lord!
  Yet not to stand secure,
Girt round with iron Pride,
  Contented to endure:
Crushing the gentle strings
  That human hearts should know,
Untouched by others' joy
  Or others' woe;—
Thou, O dear Lord, wilt never teach us so.

We ask Thy Peace, O Lord!
  Through storm, and fear, and strife,
To light and guide us on,
  Through a long, struggling life;
While no success or gain
  Shall cheer the desperate fight,
Or nerve, what the world calls
  Our wasted might:—
Yet pressing through the darkness to the light.

It is Thine own, O Lord,
  Who toil while others sleep;
Who sow with loving care
  What other hands shall reap.
They lean on Thee entranced,
  In calm and perfect rest:
Give us that Peace, O Lord,
  Divine and blest,
Thou keepest for those hearts who love
  Thee best.

Adelaide Anne Procter

LAUDA

Jesus, whoso with Thee
Hangs not in pain and loss,

Pierced on the cruel cross,
At peace shall never be.
Lord, unto me be kind;
Give me that peace of mind
Which in this world so blind
And false, dwells but with Thee.
Give me that strife and pain,
Apart from which 'twere vain
Thy love on earth to gain
Or seek a share with Thee.
If, Lord, with Thee alone
Heart's peace and love be known,
My heart shall be Thine own,
Ever to rest with Thee.
Here in my heart be lit
Thy fire, to feed on it,
Till, burning bit by bit,
It dies to live with Thee.
Jesus, whoso with Thee,
Hangs not in pain and loss,
Pierced on the cruel cross,
At peace shall never be.

Girolamo Beniveni (translated by
John Addington Symonds)

PEACE

Peace, not of earth, I ask of Thee, O God,
Peace, not in death, and yet Thy will be done;
I would not die until my soul has won
Some little grace: a barren, withered sod
My life has been,—now touch me with Thy rod,
That I may blossom, as in summer sun
Thy flowers open; pray Thee give me one
Sweet touch of peace, for I am but a clod.
I know that Thou art all and I am naught,
Yet I would show my new found love for Thee
By days all filled with striving for Thy grace.
Peace, peace, O peace! the peace which Thou hast bought

With Precious Blood for us, O give it me,
Dear Lamb of God, that I may see Thy face!

Maurice Francis Egan

"LORD, GRANT US CALM"

Lord, grant us calm, if calm can set forth Thee;
 Or tempest, if a tempest set Thee forth;
Wind from the east or west or south or north,
 Or congelation of a silent sea,
With stillness of each tremulous aspen tree.

Still let fruit fall, or hang upon the tree;
 Still let the east and west, the south and north,
Curb in their winds, or plough a thundering sea;
 Still let the earth abide to set Thee forth,
Or vanish like a smoke to set forth Thee.

Christina Rossetti

CRY FROM THE BATTLEFIELD

O Lady, together with the Child you take
In your frail arms to hush His frightened cries,
Cradle us against your heart and ache
To see the sorrow staring from our eyes.
O Lady strong beyond all ecstasy,
Young willow bent before the Breath of God,
Think still of us as little ones while we
Thrust puny chests at Heaven from this sod
And flail with futile fists against the Breast
Where beats the Beauty passion cannot taste.
O Lady, heal our wars, our dark unrest,
The lusts that lash our land a scarlet waste:
Mother of men, this bleeding face
Awaits the wonder of your love's embrace.

Robert Menth

ENGLAND'S PRAYER
(A Seventeenth Century prayer that could be uttered by and for any nation today)

Sweet Jesus with Thy Mother mild,
Sweet Virgin Mother with thy Child,
Angels and Saints of each degree,
Redress our country's misery.

Give judgment, Lord, twixt them and us,
The balance yet let pity hold,
Let mercy measure their offense
And grace reduce them to Thy fold,
That we, all children of the Spouse,
May live as brethren in Thy house.

William Blundell of Crosby

ST. MICHAEL

Come, Michael of the splendid sword,
And lead our shining hosts:
Guard us, great captain of the Lord,
Upon the embattled coasts.

Light once again our hero soul
With valor's holy fire,
Until, from out the battle goal,
We pluck the world's Desire.

Until the years of monstrous Might
For evermore shall cease;
And reigns, co-warder of the Right,
Thy brother angel, Peace.

John Jerome Rooney

From MARY OF FATIMA: A SEQUENCE

Mary, in whose frail hands
Is power made perfect—you

Whose courteous whim at Cana
Bending the mind of God
Pulled down the destiny of Christ upon Him
Before His time—hear us.
Halt the thrown stone
In the thin air, deflect
The race of man self-flung into oblivion.
Mary, changer of history,
Turn back our death!

* * * *

Oh Mary, make us pray!
Silence our whispering huddled cowardice
And crack our shelled indifference
With your atomic love!
Lady of battles and of beachheads
Conquer us into your prayer!

Virginia Earle

TO A CHRISTIAN MARTYR

Martyr of unconquered might,
Follower of the incarnate Son!
Who, victorious in the fight,
Hast celestial glory won;

By the virtue of thy prayer,
Let no evil hover nigh;
Sin's contagion drive afar;
Waken drowsy lethargy.

Roman Breviary (translated by
Edward Caswall)

ST. PATRICK'S HYMN BEFORE TARA

Christ, as a light,
Illumine and guide me!
Christ, as a shield, o'ershadow and cover me!

Christ be under me! Christ be over me!
  Christ be beside me
  On left hand and right!
Christ be before me, behind me, about me!
Christ this day be within and without me!

Christ, the lowly and meek,
  Christ, the All-powerful, be
In the heart of each to whom I speak,
  In the mouth of each who speaks to me!
  In all who draw near me,
  Or see me or hear me!

* * * *

Salvation dwells with the Lord,
With Christ, the Omnipotent Word.
From generation to generation
Grant us, O Lord, Thy grace and salvation!

James Clarence Mangan

A PRAYER FOR THE NATIONS

O God of Life and Liberty
And the Pursuit of Happiness,
Of Faith and Hope and Charity,
By which You quicken, nurse, and bless,
Look down and in Your mercy quell
The rising storm—all is not well.

When *Faith* is failing, men deny
That Life is Yours and but a loan
For us to use and profit by;
But they now claim it as their own
To choke Life at its very source
Or stop it ere it runs its course.

When *Hope* of higher things is lost,
They make of baser ones their need

To have and hold at any cost;
And so they sacrifice to greed,
With ritual of a tyrant's nod,
The Freedom of the sons of God.

When *Love* is dead, they will pursue
Their happiness in selfish gain,
While to their kind they prove untrue;
Yet all their running is in vain
When in this race they fail to find
That Happiness was left behind.

O God of Life in Faith, and of
The Liberty which Hope can know!
O God of Happiness through Love,
Have Mercy on us here below!
Send down to earth again these three:
Firm Faith, strong Hope, sweet Charity!

Fray Angelico Chavez

FOR THE HOME AND FAMILY

"UNLESS THE LORD BUILD THE HOUSE"

Unless the Lord build the house, they labour in vain that build it.
Unless the Lord keep the city, he watcheth in vain that keepeth it. . . .
Behold the inheritance of the Lord are children: the reward, the fruit of the womb.
As arrows in the hand of the mighty, so the children of them that have been shaken.

Psalm 126:1, 3–4

WEDDING HYMN

Father, within Thy House today
  We wait Thy kindly love to see;
Since Thou hast said in truth that they
  Who dwell in love are one with Thee,
Bless those who for Thy blessing wait,
  Their love accept and consecrate.

Dear Lord of love, whose Heart of Fire,
  So full of pity for our sin,
Was once in that Divine Desire
  Broken, Thy Bride to woo and win:
Look down and bless them from above
And keep their hearts alight with love.

Blest Spirit, who with life and light
  Didst quicken chaos to Thy praise,
Whose energy, in sin's despite,
  Still lifts our nature up to grace;
Bless those who here in troth consent.
  Creator, crown Thy Sacrament.

Great One-in-Three, of Whom are named
  All families in earth and heaven,
Hear us, who have Thy promise claimed,
  And let a wealth of grace be given;
Grant them in life and death to be,
  Each knit to each, and both to Thee.

Robert Hugh Benson

WEDDING HYMN

Receive this passion, rooted in the dust,
So perilous-sweet with doomed mortality,
Compounded of the flowering body's lust
And the leashed spirit's longing to be free.

It is too great to bear. To You we render
The thrusting hope, the anguish and these tears
So intricately meshed with joy—a splendor
Born of no trivial years.

Make of it what You will. Beyond our knowing
Your purpose lies, but not beyond our trust.
God, take the tenuous tribute of our growing;
Receive this passion, lifting from the dust.

Frances Stoakley Lankford

THE MAN OF THE HOUSE

Joseph, honoured from sea to sea,
This is your name that pleases me,
"Man of the House."

I see you rise at dawn and light
The fire and blow till the flame is bright.

I see you take the pitcher and carry
The deep well-water for Jesus and Mary.

You knead the corn for the bread so fine,
Gather then grapes from the hanging vine.

There are little feet that are soft and slow,
Follow you whithersoever you go.

There's a little face at your workshop door,
A little one sits down on your floor;

Holds His hands for the shavings curled,
The soft little hands that have made the world.

Mary calls you: the meal is ready:
You swing the Child to your shoulders steady.

I see your quiet smile as you sit
And watch the little Son thrive and eat.

The vine curls by the window space,
The wings of angels cover the face.

Up in the rafters, polished and olden,
There's a Dove that broods and his wings are golden.

You who kept Them through shine and storm,
A staff, and a shelter kindly and warm,

Father of Jesus, husband of Mary,
Hold us your lilies for sanctuary!

Joseph, honoured from sea to sea,
Guard me mine and my own roof-tree,
"Man of the House!"

Katharine Tynan Hinkson

PRAYER FOR A NEW HOUSE

You who spent some early days in carpentry,
Look to the building of this house,
Not to structure or to silhouette,
But to the concept shaped:
The nail is not devout,
There is nothing mystic in the saw,
Nor votive in the hammer or the awl;
Belief cannot be mortared to the beams,
Nor love secured in flooring, frame, or roof—
But You can put the heart of shelter here.

Touch this beginning—
You who knew the uses made of wood,
From manger first, through workshop, to the cross—
Put meaning here:
Set mutual faith,
As these foundation stones are set,
To be the basis of security;
And even as this door is axis to the years,
Let hope be hinge to courage.

In the name of those who live here,
Bless this house with generousness and joy.

Jo Bingham

BLESSING OF THE HOLY FAMILY

When your home is radiant, with the light
Of sunshine happiness,
May Jesus, Mary and Joseph dwell
With you to guard and bless!

If ever sorrow's dark wine sheds
Gloom on the joy-bright air,
May Jesus, Mary and Joseph bring
Comfort in your despair!

The dove of peace and the lamp of love
That burns with steadfast ray,
May Jesus, Mary and Joseph, keep
Alive in your hearts always.

Sister Mary Maura

THE MAN'S PRAYER

When all is still within these walls,
And Thy sweet sleep through darkness falls
On little hearts that trust in me,
However bitter toil may be,
For length of days, O Lord, on Thee,
My spirit calls.

Their daily need by day enthralls
My heart and brain, but when night falls
And leaves the questioning spirit free
To brood upon the days to be,
For time and strength, O Lord! on Thee
My spirit calls.

T. A. Daly

"LORD OF ALL POTS AND PANS"

Lord of all pots and pans and things; since I've no time to be
A saint by doing lovely things or watching late with Thee,
Or dreaming in the dawnlight or storming heaven's gates,
Make me a saint by getting meals, and washing up the plates.

Although I must have Martha's hands, I have a Mary mind;
And when I black the boots and shoes, Thy sandals, Lord, I find.
I think of how they trod the earth, each time I scrub the floor;
Accept this meditation, Lord, I haven't time for more.

Warm all the kitchen with Thy love, and light it with Thy peace;
Forgive me all my worrying, and make my grumbling cease.
Thou Who didst love to give men food, in room or by the sea,
Accept this service that I do—I do it unto Thee.

Anonymous

THE HOUSEWIFE'S PRAYER

Lady, who with tender word
Didst keep the house of Christ the Lord,
Who didst set forth the bread and wine
Before the Living Wheat and Vine,
Reverently didst make the bed
Whereon was laid the holy Head
That such a cruel pillow prest
For our behoof, on Calvary's crest;
Be beside me while I go
About my labors to and fro.
Speed the wheel and speed the loom,
Guide the needle and the broom,
Make my bread rise sweet and light,
Make my cheese come foamy white,
Yellow may my butter be
As cowslips blowing on the lea.
Homely though my tasks and small,
Be beside me at them all.
Then when I shall stand to face

Jesu in the judgment place,
To me thy gracious help afford,
Who art the Handmaid of the Lord.

Blanche Mary Kelly

PRAYER AT A NURSERY WINDOW

So brief a time I have them, Lord,
To steady them with Thy bright word;
A narrow span of childish days
To set their feet in Thy great ways—
A few swift nights to know them warm,
Close-gathered now from any harm,
Looming in shadowy years ahead . . .
How can I help but be afraid?

The little wisdom I have won
Is not enough to guard my son.
The grace I grope for, deed by deed,
Cannot assuage my daughter's need;
Nor wit, nor courage hold at bay
The moment, that imperiled day,
For which no foresight may prepare—
Nor even love, not even prayer.

Be to them, God, all I would be
In that far time I shall not see;
And guide me now, their friend, their mother,
To hear their prayers, to smooth the cover,
And leave their windows wide upthrust
Beneath that Heaven of my trust,
Whose pity marked a sparrow's fall
And bends in mercy over all.

Frances Stoakley Lankford

PRAYER THAT AN INFANT MAY NOT DIE

Lord, spare to them this very little child
as You preserve a grass-blade in the wind!

What will it cost You, since the mother weeps,
not to have it die there in a brief while
as a matter that cannot be avoided?
If You grant it life, it will go next year
to toss roses in the Lord's Day festival!
But You are too good! 'twould not be You, good Lord,
Who place blue death upon the rosy cheek
While there are still fine places where You can set
sons besides their mothers at the window.
But why not here? Ah, since the hour calls,
remember, Lord, before the dying child,—
You live forever at Your mother's side!

Francis Jammes (translated by Joseph T. Shipley)

OF MY DEAR SON, GERVASE BEAUMONT

Dear Lord, receive my son, whose winning love
To me was like a friendship, far above
The course of nature or his tender age;
Whose looks could all my bitter griefs assuage;
Let his pure soul, ordained seven years to be
In that frail body which was part of me,
Remain my pledge in Heaven, as sent to show
How to this port at every step I go.

Sir John Beaumont

CANDLES THAT BURN

Candles that burn for a November birthday,
Wreathed round with asters and with goldenrod,
As you go upward in your radiant dying
Carry my prayer to God.

Tell Him she is so small and rebellious,
Tell Him her words are music on her lips,
Tell Him I love her in her wayward beauty
Down to her fingertips.

Ask Him to keep her brave and true and lovely,
  Vivid and happy, gay as she is now,
Ask Him to let no shadow touch her beauty,
  Nor sorrow mar her brow.

All the sweet saints that came for her baptizing,
  Tell them I pray them to be always near.
Ask them to keep her little feet from stumbling,
  Her gallant heart from fear.

Candles that burn for a November birthday,
  Wreathed round with asters and with goldenrod,
As you go upward in your radiant dying,
  Carry my prayer to God.

Aline Kilmer

FOR SPECIAL PURPOSES, OCCASIONS, AND PEOPLE

From HYMN FOR THE CHURCH MILITANT

Lord, when we cry Thee far and near
And thunder through all lands unknown
The gospel into every ear,
Lord, let us not forget our own.

Cleanse us from ire of creed or class,
The anger of the idle kings;
Sow in our souls, like living grass,
The laughter of all lowly things.

G. K. Chesterton

A HYMN

O God of earth and altar,
  Bow down and hear our cry,
Our earthly rulers falter,
  Our people drift and die;
The walls of gold entomb us,
  The swords of scorn divide us,
Take not thy thunder from us,
  But take away our pride.

From all that terror teaches,
  From lies of tongue and pen,
From all the easy speeches
  That comfort cruel men,
For sale and profanation
  Of honour and the sword,
From sleep and from damnation,
  Deliver us, good Lord.

Tie in a living tether
  The prince and priest and thrall,
Bind all our lives together,
  Smite us and save us all;

In ire and exultation
  Aflame with faith, and free,
Lift up a living nation,
  A single sword to thee.

G. K. Chesterton

"LORD, WHILE FOR ALL MANKIND WE PRAY"

Lord, while for all mankind we pray
Of every clime and coast,
O hear us for our native land,
The land we love the most.

O guard our shores from every foe;
With peace our borders bless;
With prosp'rous times our cities crown,
Our fields with plenteousness.

Unite us in the sacred love
Of knowledge, truth and Thee,
And let our hills and valleys shout
The songs of liberty.

Lord of the nations, thus to Thee
Our country we commend;
Be Thou our refuge and our trust,
Her everlasting friend.

John Wreford

JOSEPH OF DREAMS

Joseph of dreams, guard well the poor.
Be a strong bar upon the door.
Be a broad window all day long
To let in sun and wild bird song.
Set a new loaf upon the board
to fill the poor man's scanty board.

With strength and patience bless the lives
of all poor men and poor men's wives.
Listen to poor men's children call
when they are cold and tired and small.
Stir up the fire and keep it bright
on poor men's hearths at fall of night.
Build a dry roof above the heads
of poor men dreaming in their beds.
Bring peace to all poor souls who lie
afraid and lonely when they die.
Joseph of dreams, in that last hour
be a great light, be a strong tower.

Sister Maris Stella

FRIENDS

O patron Saints of all my friends!
O guardian Angels of them all!
With them begins, with them still ends,
My prayer's most passionate call.

You know my voice: you know their names,
That wing so its least selfish tone
Across your white celestial flames,
And up to the White Throne.

Heaven were not Heaven, and they were not there;
Heaven were no Heaven, my friends away:
O Saints and Angels! hear my prayer,
I pray you every day.

Lionel Johnson

ST. ANTHONY'S CLIENT

How many times, O sweet Saint Anthony!
When precious little things were lost, mislaid,
How many trusting times, I've turned to thee,
And tenderly sought thy potent aid.

And never yet in vain—a glove—a ring—
A book—a *reliquaire*—a rosary—
Each trifling trinket—yea, each treasur'd thing,
Thy gracious care hath given back to me.

Thanks, gentle saint—Ah! yet once more, extend
Thy loving aid; for I have lost today
That treasure of all treasured things—a friend,
Whom some perverse misdoubt hath led astray.

Dearer than book, or ring, or perfum'd glove!
Rarer than rosary or *reliquaire*—
Of all earth's missing things, shall missing love
Alone, alas! be lost beyond repair?

Must malice wound, or misconstruction sour
The sweetest of all spirits to the end?
Ah! no, Saint Anthony! exert thy power,
And give, oh! give me back my dear lost friend!

Eleanor C. Donnelly

CADGWITH

III

Mary Star of the sea!
Look on this little place:
Bless the kind fisher race,
Mary Star of the sea!

Send harvest from the deep,
Mary Star of the sea!
Mary Star of the sea!
Let not these women weep.

Mary Star of the sea!
Give wife and mother joy

In husband and in boy:
Mary Star of the sea!

With intercession save,
Mary Star of the sea!
Mary Star of the sea!
These children of the wave.

Mary Star of the sea!
Pour peace upon the wild
Waves, make their murmurs mild:
Mary Star of the sea!

Now in thy mercy pray,
Mary Star of the sea!
Mary Star of the sea!
For sailors far away.

Mary Star of the sea!
Now be thy great prayers said
For all poor seamen dead:
Mary Star of the sea!

Lionel Johnson

THE TEACHER

Lord, who am I to teach the way
To little children day by day,
So prone myself to go astray?

I teach them KNOWLEDGE, but I know
How faint they flicker and how low
The candles of my knowledge glow.

I teach them POWER to will and do,
But only now to learn anew
My own great weakness through and through.

I teach them LOVE for all mankind
And all God's creatures, but I find
My love comes lagging far behind.

Lord, if their guide I still must be,
Oh, let the little children see
The teacher leaning hard on Thee.

Leslie Pinckney Hill

PRAYER FOR A TRAVELLER

Father, Son, and Paraclete,
Mary, Joseph, John,
Guard your heart and guide your feet
Now till set of sun.

Bring you to that family-seat
Christ for us has won—
Father, Son and Paraclete,
Mary, Joseph, John!

Charles L. O'Donnell

GRACE BEFORE PLANTING IN WARTIME
(For Brother Richards, C.P.)

God, in this bitter hour
   When skies are dark with doom,
By Thy Almighty power
Bring Thou this seed to flower:
   Bless leaf and bud and bloom.

Thou Grain and Growth, and Grower,
   Thou, Godhead, Three in One,
Bless seed and sod and sower,
Bless scythe and sheaf and mower,
   Bless worker and work done.

James L. Duff

PRAYER
(To be said when putting on one's coat)

Keep Thou, O Lord, my going out,
  And keep Thou, too, my coming in;
With Thy love compass me about
  To keep me safe and free from sin.

Bless Thou my going out, and bless
  All those whom I may chance to meet;
Wherever I go, let men confess
  That Thou art good, and virtue sweet.

Bless Thou my coming in; and when
  I come, come Thou, dear Lord, with me
That men may feel Thee near—and then
  Bless all the gathered company.

Bless me and this garment which I wear
  When I go out, when I come in;
Forth then into the world I'll fare
  And come back safe and free from sin.

Ruth Mary Fox

ONLY FOR TODAY, LORD

Only for today, Lord, only for today,
  Let the days hereafter
  Sorrow bring or laughter:
  How *that* dies away—
Only for today, Lord, strength just for today.

Fallen are my castles, air-built, crystal-fair,
  Ah, they were erected,
  Not a stone neglected—
  With such tender care:
Build of golden vapour, built on purple air!

Oh, my airy mansions! Oh, the loving hands!
  Oh, the tender dreaming!
  See how fails our scheming—
  All our plots and plans—
Oh, my airy mansions, built with loving hands!

Nevermore to dream, Lord, only just to live
  From still hour to hour,
  As live grass or flower,
  Sure this boon Thou'lt give—
Nevermore to dream, Lord, only just to live.

Nevermore with eager eyes toward the sun,
  Breast the purple ether,
  Oh, the Summer weather
  When that flight begun!
Sometime wings are broken soaring to the sun.

Eleanor Cox

WHO SHALL DELIVER ME?

God strengthen me to bear myself;
That heaviest weight of all to bear,
Inalienable weight of care,

All others are outside myself;
I lock my door and bar them out,
The turmoil, tedium, gad-about.

I lock my door upon myself,
And bar them out; but who shall wall
Self from myself, most loathed of all?

If I could once lay down myself,
And start self-purged upon the race
That all must run! Death runs apace.

If I could set aside myself,
And start with lightened heart upon
The road by all men overgone!

God harden me against myself,
This coward with pathetic voice
Who craves for ease, and rest, and joys:

Myself, arch-traitor to myself;
My hollowest friend, my deadliest foe,
My clog whatever road I go.

Yet One there is can curb myself,
Can roll the strangling load from me,
Break off the yoke and set me free.

Christina Rossetti

BALLADE OF A VOICE CRYING

Archangel, herald, guardian and page,
Alert to twisted tongue proclaiming views,
To teeth which all too rarely clamp, in cage
Of prudence, words bit short, too often bruise
With fanged impress—O Gabriel, this age
Needs your reminder to make daily muse
Upon the date of judgment and to gauge
How far man's progress past primeval ooze.

Scanner of printed and of mute message,
Of open insult and of secret ruse,
Of whispered rumor and of headline rage,
Proofreader of those metal hearts which choose
To transpose truth, lisp lies, under umbrage
Of need to invert virtue, vend venom, lose
All sight of soul—O Gabriel, most sage:
How far man's progress past primeval ooze?

Rover and guardian of sky's resplendent stage,
Beneath its angeled areas still brews
Hate imitating Lucifer: to wage
Chaotic war, dim sun, ban stars, the hues
Of harmony drain and erase, courage

Distort, all honor maim, beauty abuse—
O Gabriel, the Most High calm, assuage:
How far man's progress past primeval ooze!

Envoy
Prince of Communication, Word image,
Whose tidings brought to waiting earth Good News,
Unclog choked channels and assure this age
How far man's progress past primeval ooze.

James Edward Tobin

TO SAINT MARGARET

Fair Amazon of Heaven who tookst in hand
Saint Michael and Saint George to imitate,
And for a tyrant's love transformed to hate
Wast for thy lily faith retained in band,
Alone on foot and with thy naked hand
Thou didst like Michael and his host; and that
For which on horse armed George we celebrate
Whilst Thou, like them, a dragon didst withstand.
Behold my soul shut in my body's gaol,
The which the Drake of Hell gapes to devour.
Teach me (O virgin) how thou didst prevail.
Virginity, thou sayest, was all thy aid:
Give me then purity instead of power,
And let my soul, made chaste, pass for a Maid.

Henry Constable

TO OUR LADY

O Lady leal and lovesomest,
Thy face most fair and sheen is!
O blossom blithe and buxomest,
From carnal crime that clean is!
This prayer from my spleen is,
That all my works wickedest

Thou put away and make me chaste
From Termagent that teen* is
And from this claw that keen is;
And syne till heaven my soul thou hast
Where thy Maker of mightiness most
Is King and thou their Queen is!

Robert Henryson

PRO CASTITUE

Virgin, born of Virgin,
To thy shelter take me;
Purest, holiest Jesu,
Chaste and holy make me.

Wisdom, power and beauty,
These are not for me;
Give me, give me only
Perfect chastity.

. . .

Keep my flesh and spirit,
Eyes and ears and speech,
Taste and touch and feeling,
Sanctifying them each.

Through the fiery furnace
Walk, O Love, beside me;
In the provocation
From the tempter hide me.

. . .

Not for might and glory
Do I ask above,
Seeking of Thee only
Love and love and love.

Digby Mackworth Dolben

---

* Grief

FOR MERCY

"HAVE MERCY ON ME, O GOD"

Have mercy on me, O God, according to thy great mercy.
And according to the multitude of thy tender mercies blot out my iniquity.
Wash me yet more from my iniquity, and cleanse me from my sin.
For I know my iniquity, and my sin is always before me. . . .
Turn away thy face from my sins, and blot out all my iniquities.
Create a clean heart in me, O God: and renew a right spirit within my bowels.
Cast me not away from thy face; and take not thy holy spirit from me.
Restore unto me the joy of thy salvation, and strengthen me with a perfect spirit.

Psalm 50:3–5, 11–14

FORGIVENESS AND MERCY

Jesu Christ, have mercy on me,
As thou art king of majesty,

And forgive me my sins all
That I have done, both great and small.

And bring me, if it be thy will,
Till heaven, to live aye with thee still. Amen.

Richard Rolle

GOD

Have mercy on us, God most high!
  Who lift our hearts to Thee,
Have mercy on us worms of earth,
  Most holy Trinity!

Most ancient of all mysteries!
  Before Thy throne we lie;
Have mercy now, most merciful,
  Most holy Trinity!

Frederick W. Faber

TE DEUM

Thee, Sovereign God, our grateful Accents praise;
We own thee Lord, and bless thy wondrous ways;
To thee, Eternal Father, Earth's whole Frame
With loudest Trumpets sounds immortal Fame. . . .
Thou King of Glory, Christ, of the Most High
Thou co-eternal Filial Deity;
Thou who, to save the World's impending Doom,
Vouchsaf'dst to dwell within a Virgin's Womb;
Old Tyrant Death disarm'd, before thee flew
The Bolts of Heav'n, and back the Foldings drew,
To give access, and make thy faithful way;
From God's right Hand thy filial Beams display.

Thou art to judge the Living and the Dead;
Then spare those Souls for whom thy Veins have bled.
O take us up among thy blest above,
To share with them thy everlasting Love.
Preserve, O Lord! thy People, and enhance
Thy Blessing on thine own Inheritance.
For ever raise their Hearts, and rule their ways,
Each day we bless thee, and proclaim thy Praise;
No Age shall fail to celebrate thy Name,
No Hour neglect thy everlasting Fame.
Preserve our Souls, O Lord, this Day from Ill;
Have Mercy on us, Lord, have Mercy still:
As we have hop'd, do thou reward our Pain;
We've hop'd in thee, let not our Hope be vain.

Translated by John Dryden

TO THE TRINITY

Trinity blessed, Deity coequal,
Unity sacred, God one eke in essence,
Yield to Thy servant, pitifully calling
Merciful hearing.

Virtuous living did I long relinquish,
Thy will and precepts miserably scorning,
Grant to me, sinful patient, repenting,
Healthful amendment.

Richard Stanyhurst

LITANY TO THE HOLY SPIRIT

In the hour of my distress,
When temptations me oppress,
And when I my sins confess,
Sweet Spirit comfort me!

When I lie within my bed,
Sick in heart, and sick in head,

And with doubts discomforted,
Sweet Spirit comfort me!

When the house doth sigh and weep,
And the world is drown'd in sleep,
Yet mine eyes the watch do keep;
Sweet Spirit comfort me! . . .

When the passing-bell doth toll,
And the furies in a shoal
Come to fright a parting soul;
Sweet Spirit comfort me!

When the tapers now burn blue,
And the comforters are few,
And that number more than true;
Sweet Spirit comfort me!

When the priest his last hath pray'd,
And I nod to what is said,
'Cause my speech is now decayed;
Sweet Spirit comfort me!

When (God knows) I'm toss'd about,
Either with despair, or doubt;
Yet before the glass be out,
Sweet Spirit comfort me!

When the tempter me pursu'th
With the sins of all my youth,
And half damns me with untruth;
Sweet Spirit comfort me!

When the flames and hellish cries
Fright mine ears, and fright mine eyes,
And all terrors me surprise;
Sweet Spirit comfort me!

When the judgment is reveal'd,
And that open'd which was seal'd,

When to Thee I have appeal'd;
Sweet Spirit comfort me!

Robert Herrick

DISCIPLINE

Throw away thy rod,
Throw away thy wrath:
  O My God,
Take the gentle path.

For my heart's desire
Unto thine is bent:
  I aspire
To a full consent.

Not a word or look
I affect to own,
  But by book,
And thy Book alone.

Though I fail, I weep:
Though I halt in pace,
  Yet I creep
To the throne of grace.

Then let wrath remove;
Love will do the deed:
  For with love
  Stony hearts will bleed.

Love is swift on foot;
Love's a man of war,
  And can shoot,
And can hit from far.

Who can scape his bow?
That which wrought on thee,

Brought thee low,
Needs must work on me.

Throw away thy rod;
Though man frailties hath,
Thou art God:
Throw away thy wrath.

George Herbert

"REMEMBER NOT, LORD, MY SINS"

Remember not, Lord, my sins,
nor the sins of my forefathers;
neither take vengeance for our sins, theirs, nor mine.
Spare us, Lord, them and me,
spare Thy people,
and, among Thy people, Thy servant,
who is redeemed with Thy precious blood;
and be not angry with us for ever.
Be merciful, be merciful; spare us, Lord,
and be not angry with us, for ever.
Be merciful, be merciful; have pity on us, Lord,
and be not angry with us to the full.
Deal not, O Lord,
deal not with me after mine iniquities,
neither recompense me according to my sins;
but after Thy great pity,
deal with me,
and according to the multitude of Thy mercies,
recompense me
after that so great pity,
and that multitude of mercies,
as Thou didst to our fathers
in the times of old;—
by all that is dear unto Thee.

Lancelot Andrewes (translated by
John Henry Newman)

STIGMATA

In the wrath of the lips that assail us,
 In the scorn of the lips that are dumb,
The symbols of sorrow avail us,
 The joy of the people is come.
They parted Thy garments for barter,
 They follow Thy steps with complaint;
Let them know that the pyre of the martyr
 But purges the blood of the saint!

They have crucified Thee for a token,
 For a token Thy flesh crucified
Shall bleed in a heart that is broken
 For love of the wound in Thy side;
In pity for palms that were pleading,
 For feet that were grievously used,
There is blood on the brow that is bleeding
 And torn, as Thy brow that was bruised!
By Thee have we life, breath, and being;
 Thou hast knowledge of us and our kind;
Thou hast pleasure of eyes that are seeing,
And sorrow of eyes that are blind;
By the seal of the mystery shown us—
 The wound that with Thy wounds accord—
O Lord, have mercy upon us!
 Have mercy upon us, O Lord!

Charles Warren Stoddard

THE GOOD SHEPHERD

 Shepherd! who with thine amorous, sylvan song
Hast broken the slumber that encompassed me,
Who mad'st Thy crook from the accursèd tree
On which Thy powerful arms were stretched so long!
 Lead me to mercy's ever-flowing fountains;
For Thou my shepherd, guard, and guide shall be;
I will obey Thy voice, and wait to see

Thy feet all beautiful upon the mountains.
Hear Shepherd, Thou who for Thy flock art dying,
Oh, wash away these scarlet sins, for Thou
Rejoicest at the contrite sinner's vow!
Oh, wait! to Thee my weary soul is crying,
Wait for me! Yet why ask it, when I see,
With feet nailed to the cross, Thou'rt still waiting for me!

Lope de Vega (translated by
Henry Wadsworth Longfellow)

SIGHS AND GROANS

Do not use me
After my sins! look not on my desert,
But on thy glory! then thou wilt reform,
And not refuse me: for thou only art
The mighty God, but I a silly worm:
O do not bruise me!

O do not urge me!
For what account can thy ill steward make?
I have abus'd thy flock, destroy'd thy woods,
Sucked all thy magazines: my head did ache,
Till it found out how to consume thy goods:
O do not scourge me!

O do not blind me!
I have deserv'd that an Egyptian night
Should thicken all my powers; because my lust
Hath still sow'd fig-leaves to exclude thy light:
But I am frailty, and already dust:
O do not grind me!

O do not fill me
With the turn'd vial of thy bitter wrath!
For thou hast other vessels full of blood,
A part whereof my Saviour emptied hath,
Ev'n unto death: since he died for my good,
O do not kill me!

But O reprieve me!
For thou hast life and death at thy command;
Thou art both Judge and Saviour, feast and rod,
Cordial and Corrosive: put not thy hand
Into the bitter box; but O my God,
My God, relieve me!

George Herbert

AN OUTDOOR LITANY

Domec misereatur nostri.

The spur is red upon the briar,
The sea-kelp whips the wave ashore;
The wind shakes out the coloured fire
From lamps a-row on the sycamore;
The bluebird with his flitting note
Shows to wild heaven his wedding coat;
The mink is busy; herds again
Go hillward in the honeyed rain;
The midges meet. I cry to Thee
Whose heart
Remembers each of these: Thou art
My God who hast forgotten me!

Bright from the mast, a scarf unwound,
The lined gulls in the offing ride;
Along an edge of marshy ground
The shad-bush enters like a bride.
Yon little clouds are washed of care
That climb the blue New England air,
And almost merrily withal
The hyla tunes at evenfall
His oboe in a mossy tree.
So too,
Am I not Thine? Arise, undo
This fear Thou hast forgotten me.

Happy the vernal rout that come
To their due offices to-day,

And strange, if in Thy mercy's sum,
Excluded man alone decay.
I ask no triumph, ask no joy,
Save leave to live, in law's employ.
As to a weed, to me but give
Thy sap! lest aye inoperative
Here in the Pit my strength shall be:
And still
Help me endure the Pit, until
Thou wilt not have forgotten me.

Louise Imogen Guiney

"A LITTLE WHILE . . ."

A thousand years to You are as a day,
Eternal One: yet knowing human tears
And fears, forget not the heart's limping way
When days may linger as a thousand years!

Katherine Brégy

KYRIE ELEISON

In joy, in pain, in sorrow,
Father, Thy hand we see;
But some among Thy children
Deny this Faith and Thee.
They will not ask Thy mercy,
But we kneel for them in prayer;
Are they not still Thy children?
Pity, O God! and spare.
Thy peace, O Lord, has never
On their desolate pathway shone,
Darkness is all around them,
Kyrie Eleison!

. . .

By the love Thy saints have shown Thee,
And the sorrows they have borne,

Leave not these erring creatures
  To wander thus forlorn.
By Thy tender name of Saviour,—
  The name they have denied;
By Thy bitter death and passion,
  And the Cross which they deride;
By the anguish Thou hast suffered,
  And the glory Thou hast won;
By Thy love and by Thy pity—
  Christe Eleison!

Pray for them glorious seraphs,
  And ye, bright angel band,
Who chant His praises ever,
  And in His presence stand;
And thou, O gentle Mother,
  Queen of the starry sky;
Ye Saints whose toils are over,
  Join your voices to our cry,—
In Thy terror or Thy mercy,
  Call them ere life is done,
For His sake Who died to save them,
  Kyrie Eleison!

Adelaide Anne Procter

AGAINST DESPAIR

You are Treasure, Lord, beyond all price,
I needs must tell You as the pledge I lay
Against that bitter and regretful day
When I might well deny You more than thrice.

And lest I be as so much sifted wheat,
Oh, pray no grain by any wind shall blow
Beyond the magnet of Your eyes, or go
Outside the reach of pinioned hands and feet.

Or should I sell You, and the price be set
At thirty silver pieces, more or less,

Oh, let me not forget in my distress
The heart I battered will receive me yet.

Sister Mary Ada

BEFORE THE BEGINNING

Before the beginning Thou hast foreknown the end,
Before the birthday the death-bed was seen of Thee:
Cleanse what I cannot cleanse, mend what I cannot mend,
O Lord All-Merciful, be merciful to me.

While the end is drawing near I know not mine end;
Birth I recall not, my death I cannot foresee:
O God, arise to defend, arise to befriend,
O Lord All-Merciful, be merciful to me.

Christina Rossetti

"THY SERVANT DELIVER"

Be merciful, be gracious, spare him, Lord.
Be merciful, be gracious, Lord, deliver him.
From the sins that are past;
From Thy frowns and Thine ire;
From the perils of dying;
From any complying
With sin, or denying
His God, or relying
On self, at the last;
From the nethermost fire;
From all that is evil;
From power of the devil;
Thy servant deliver,
For once and for ever.

John Henry Newman

ALL SOULS' EVE

Wild the sea clamors from its echoing caves,
But other voices rise above the waves:

"As now you are, O friends, so once we were;
As now we are, so one day you shall be!"
And still they rise and plead and hurry by,
Sobbing and breaking in that long, sad cry—
"Orate pro nobis!"

Father of all, be merciful to all!
Hold not these faithful servants long in thrall;
Open to them Thy blessed dwelling-place,
Hide not too long the glory of Thy face.
Mother of pity, harken to that cry,
Cleaving the clouds, and quivering to the sky—
"Orate pro nobis!"

Mary E. Mannix

THE LAST DAYS, AND AFTER

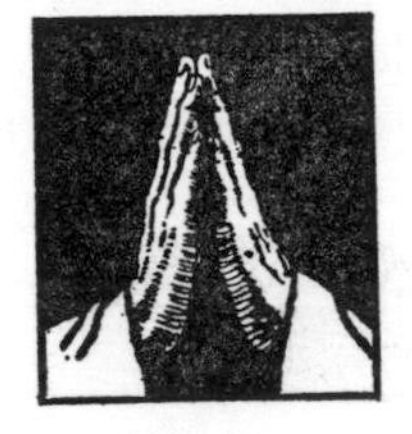

"O GOD, COME TO MY ASSISTANCE"

O God, come to my assistance; O Lord, make haste to help me.
Let them be confounded and ashamed that seek my soul: . . .
Let all that seek thee rejoice and be glad in thee; and let such as love
thy salvation say always: The Lord be magnified.
But I am needy and poor; O God, help me.
Thou art my helper and deliverer: O Lord, make no delay.

Psalm 69:2–3, 5–6

From *DIES IRAE*

Thou, O awe-inspiring Lord,
Saving e'en when unimplored,
Save me, mercy's fount adored.

Ah! Sweet Jesus, mindful be,
That Thou cam'st on earth for me:
Cast me not this day from Thee.

Seeking me Thy strength was spent,
Ransoming Thy limbs were rent:
Is this toil to no intent?

Thou, awarding pains condign,
Mercy's ear to me incline,
Ere the reckoning Thou assign.

I, felon-like, my lot bewail,
Suffused cheeks my shame unveil:
God! O let my prayer prevail.

Mary's soul Thou madest white,
Didst to heaven the thief invite;
Hope in me these now excite. . . .

Place amid Thy sheep accord,
Keep me from the tainted horde,
Set me in Thy sight, O Lord.

Prostrate, suppliant, now no more,
Unrepenting, as of yore,
Save me dying, I implore.

Roman Missal, For All Souls' Day

A PRAYER

From falsehood and error,
From darkness and terror,
From all that is evil,

From the power of the devil,
From the fire and the doom,
From the judgment to come
Sweet Jesu, deliver
Thy servants forever.

Digby Mackworth Dolben

WISHES

I wish to have no wishes left,
But to leave all to Thee;
And yet I wish that Thou shouldst will
Things that I wish should be.

And these two wills I feel within,
As on my death I muse;
But, Lord! I have a death to die,
And not a death to choose.

Frederick W. Faber

A LAST PRAYER

Father, I scarcely dare to pray,
So clear I see, now it is done,
That I have wasted half my day,
And left my work but just begun;

So clear I see that things I thought
Were right or harmless were a sin;
So clear I see that I have sought
Unconscious, selfish aims to win;

So clear I see that I have hurt
The soul I might have helped to save;
That I have slothful been, inert,
Deaf to the calls thy leaders gave.

In outskirts of thy kingdom vast,
Father, the humblest spot give me;

Set me the lowliest task thou hast:
Let me repentant work for Thee!

Helen Hunt Jackson

HORA NOVISSIMA

Whene'er goes forth Thy dread command,
And my last hour is nigh,
Lord, grant me in a Christian land,
As I was born, to die.

I pray not, Lord, that friends may be,
Or kindred, standing by,
Choice blessing! which I leave to Thee
To grant me or deny.

But let my failing limbs beneath
My Mother's smile recline;
And prayers sustain my laboring breath
From out her Sacred shrine.

And let the Cross beside my bed
In its due emblem rest:
And let the absolving words be said,
To ease a laden breast.

Thou, Lord, where'er we lie, canst aid;
But He, who taught His own
To live as one, will not upbraid
The dread to die alone.

John Henry Newman

GOD

God be in my head
And in my understanding;
God be in my eyes
And in my looking;

God be in my mouth;
And in my speaking;
God be in my heart
And in my thinking:
God be at my end
And at my departing.

Anonymous

E TENEBRIS

Come down, O Christ, and help me! reach thy hand,
For I am drowning in a stormier sea
Than Simon on thy Lake of Galilee:
The wine of life is spilt upon the sand,
My heart is as some famine-murdered land
When all good things have perished utterly,
And well I know my soul in Hell must lie
If I this night before God's throne should stand.
"He sleeps perchance, or rideth to the chase,
Like Baal, when his prophets howled that name
From morn till noon on Carmel's smitten height."
Nay, peace, I shall behold before the night,
The feet of brass, the robe more white than flame,
The wounded hands, the weary human face.

Oscar Wilde

THE FATHER

Father of Heaven, and him, by whom
It, and us for it, and all else, for us
Thou madest, and govern'st ever, come
And re-create me, now grown ruinous:
My heart is by dejection, clay,
And by self-murder, red.
From this red earth, O Father, purge away
All vicious tinctures, that new fashioned
I may rise up from death, before I'm dead.

John Donne

DAY OF JUDGMENT

When through the North a fire shall rush
And roll into the East,
And like a fiery torrent brush
And sweep up South and West,

When all shall stream and lighten round
And with surprising flames
Both stars and elements confound
And quite blot out their names,

When Thou shalt spend Thy sacred store
Of thunders in that heat
And low as ere they lay before
Thy six-days' buildings beat,

When like a scroll the heavens shall pass
And vanish clean away,
And naught must stand of that vast space
Which held up night and day,

When one loud blast shall rend the deep
And from the womb of earth
Summon up all that are asleep
Unto a second birth,

When Thou shalt make the clouds Thy seat,
And in the open air
Thy quick and dead, both small and great,
Must to Thy bar repair;

O then it will be all too late
To say, What shall I do?
Repentance there is out of date
And so is mercy too;

Prepare, prepare me then, O God!
And let me now begin

To feel my loving Father's rod
Killing the man of sin!

Give me, O give me crosses here,
Still more afflictions lend;
That pill, though bitter, is most dear
That brings health in the end;

Lord, God! I beg nor friends nor wealth,
But pray against them both;
Three things I'd have, my soul's chief health!
And one of these seem loath,

A living faith, a heart of flesh,
The world an enemy;
This last will keep the first two fresh,
And bring me where I'd be.

Henry Vaughan

THE PROPHET LOST IN THE HILLS AT EVENING

Strong God which made the topmost stars
To circulate and keep their course,
Remember me; whom all the bars
Of sense and dreadful fate enforce.

Above me in your heights and tall,
Impassable the summits freeze,
Below the haunted waters call
Impassable beyond the trees.

I hunger and I have no bread.
My gourd is empty of the wine.
Surely the footsteps of the dead
Are shuffling softly close to mine!

It darkens. I have lost the ford.
There is a change on all things made.

The rocks have evil faces, Lord,
And I am awfully afraid.

Remember me! the Voids of Hell
Expand enormous all around,
Strong friends of souls, Emmanuel,
Redeem me from accursed ground.

The long descent of wasted days,
To these at last have led me down;
Remember that I filled with praise
The meaningless and doubtful ways
That lead to an eternal town.

I challenged and I kept the Faith,
The bleeding path alone I trod;
It darkens. Stand about my wraith,
And harbour me—almighty God!

Hilaire Belloc

WHEN, WHERE AND HOW?

Dear Lord, in some dim future year,
In some dim future month and day,
Abides the hour, the solemn hour
When Thou shalt call my soul away,
That year, that month, that day of days,
Come soon? come late?—I know not when.
O Thou, who rulest all my ways!
Master of life, whom Death obeys,
Be with me then, be with me then!

Somewhere upon this globe of ours,
Is hid the spot where I must die,
Where 'mid the snows, or 'mid the flowers,
My shrouded form shall coffin'd lie.
If north or south? If east or west?
At home? abroad?—I know not where.

O tender Father, Lord of grace!
Whose presence fills the realms of space,
Be with me there, be with me there!

By fire? by flood? by famine sore?
By sudden stroke? by slow decay?
When Death's dark angel opes my door.
How shall it call my soul away:
God only knows: HE bends the bow,
And He alone can fix the dart.
Yet care I not when, where, or how
The end may come, sweet Lord! if Thou
Wilt then but shield me in Thy Heart!

Eleanor C. Donnelly

"WHILST I DWELL, O MY GOD, IN THIS VALLEY OF TEARS"

Whilst I dwell, O my God, in this valley of tears,
For refuge and comfort I fly unto Thee;
And when death's awful hour with it's terrors appears,
O merciful Jesus, have mercy on me.

William Young

ABIDE WITH ME

Abide with me! fast falls the eventide;
The darkness deepens: Lord, with me abide!
When other helpers fail, and comforts flee,
Help of the helpless, O abide with me!

Swift to its close ebbs out life's little day;
Earth's joys grow dim, its glories pass away;
Change and decay in all around I see:
O Thou who changest not, abide with me!

I need Thy presence every passing hour:
What but Thy grace can foil the tempter's power?

Who like Thyself my guide and stay can be?
Through cloud and sunshine, O abide with me!

I fear no foe, with Thee at hand to bless:
Ills have no weight, and tears no bitterness:
Where is death's sting? where, grave, thy victory?
I triumph still, if Thou abide with me!

Hold Thou Thy cross before my closing eyes;
Shine through the gloom and point me to the skies;
Heaven's morning breaks, and earth's vain shadows flee
In life, in death, O Lord, abide with me!

Henry Francis Lyte

AT DEATH

Christ, unconquered King of glory!
Thou my wretched soul relieve
In that most extreme terror
When the body she must leave:
Let the accuser of the brethren
O'er me then no power receive!

St. Peter Damian (translated by J. M. Neale)

SACRIFICE

If my feeble prayer can reach Thee,
O, my Saviour, I beseech Thee,
Even as Thou hast died for me
More sincerely
Let me follow where Thou leadest,
Let me bleeding as Thou bleedest,
Die, if dying I may give
Life to one who asks to live;
And more nearly
Dying thus, resemble Thee.

Anonymous

QUI RENOVAT JUVENTUTUM MEAM

Make me grow young again,
Grow young enough to die,
That, in a joy unseared of pain,
I may, my Lover, love attain,
With that fresh sigh
Eternity
Gives to the young to breathe about the heart,
Until their trust in youth-time shall depart.

Let me be young as when
To die was past my thought;
And earth with straight immortal men,
And women deathless to my ken,
Cast fear to nought!
Let faith be fraught,
My Bridegroom, with such gallant love, its range
Simply surpasses every halt of change!

Let me come to Thee young,
When Thou dost challenge *Come!*
With all my marvelling dreams unsung,
Their promise by first passion stung,
Though chary, dumb . . .
Thou callest *Come!*
Let me rush to Thee when I pass,
Keen as a child across the grass.

Michael Field

IN EXTREMIS

Lord, as from Thy body bleeding,
Wave by wave is life receding.
From these limbs of mine,
As it drifts away from me
To the everlasting sea,
Blind it, Lord, with Thine.

John Banister Tabb

THE OLD PASTOR

How long, O Lord, to wait
Beside this open gate?
My sheep with many a lamb
Have entered, and I am
Alone, and it is late.

John Banister Tabb

A PRAYER *FOR* DEATH

Absent from thee, my Saviour dear,
I call not life this living here,
But a long dying agony,
The sharpest I have known;
And I myself, myself to see
In such a wrack of misery,
For very pity moan;
And ever, ever, weep and sigh,
Dying because I do not die.

Ah! Lord, my light and living breath,
Take me, Oh, take me from this death,
And burst the bars that sever me
From my true life above!
Think how I die thy face to see,
And cannot live away from thee,
O my eternal Love.
And ever, ever, weep and sigh,
Dying, because I do not die.

St. Teresa of Avila (translated by Edward Caswall)

"WHAT HAVE I LEFT?"

What have I left, that I should stay and groan?
The most to me to heav'n is fled:
My thoughts and joys are all packed up and gone,

And for their old acquaintance plead.
O show thy self to me,
Or take me up to thee!

George Herbert

"NEVER WEATHER-BEATEN SAIL"

Never weather-beaten sail more willing bent to shore,
Never tired pilgrim's limbs affected slumber more,
Than my wearied spirit now longs to fly out of my troubled breast:
O come quickly, sweetest Lord, and take my soul to rest!

Ever blooming are the joys of Heaven's high Paradise,
Cold age deafs not there our ears nor vapor dims our eyes:
Glory there the sun outshines; whose beams the Blessed only see:
O come quickly, glorious Lord, and raise my sprite to Thee!

Thomas Campion

LET MINE EYES SEE THEE

Let mine eyes see Thee,
Sweet Jesus of Nazareth,
Let mine eyes see Thee,
And then see death.

Let them see that care
Roses and jessamine:
Seeing Thy face most fair
All blossoms are therein.

Flower of seraphim,
Sweet Jesus of Nazareth,
Let mine eyes see Thee,
And then see death.

Nothing I require
Where my Jesus is;

Anguish all desire,
Saving only this;
All my help is His,
He only succoreth.

Let mine eyes see Thee,
Sweet Jesus of Nazareth,
Let mine eyes see Thee and then see death.

St. Teresa of Avila (translated by Arthur Symons)

PRAYER BEFORE EXECUTION

O merciful Father! my hope is in Thee!
O gracious Redeemer, deliver Thou me!
My bondage bemoaning, with sorrowful groaning,
I long to be free;
Lamenting, relenting, and humbly repenting,
O Jesus, my Saviour, I languish for Thee!

Mary Queen of Scots (translated by John Fawcett)

THE HOLY *VIATICUM* COMES TO ME

Thou Lord of Life and glorious King of Heaven,
Thou by the world, the universe, adored,
In Thy mysterious veil Thou now hast given
To me Thy presence, as my prayer implored.
I thank Thee, God, the aspiring soul is even
One instant languishing and now restored.
As grass in earth, to be from its root riven,
Thou canst my death decree, for Thou art Lord.
So be it as Thou wilt; to Thy kind care,
If I must die, my dear ones I consign,
Whom now I cannot name with tearless eyes,
Let not my daughter's steps the foe ensnare,
But guide her lovingly in ways divine.
I pardon all and thus Thy pardon prize.

Giovanni Prati (translated by Florence Trail)

PRAY FOR ME, MOTHER OF GOD!

Pray for me, Mother of God! To you I cry,
Pray for me, Mother, now and the hour I die.

O if too weak to call on your darling name
When the now and the hour of my death are one and the same,

Failing of tongue, as failing of eye and of ear,
Still on the beat of my heart my Mother shall hear,

Sweetest of names e'er given to the earth save one,
Mother of mine, your name with the name of your Son.

Jesus! Mary! O dearest and lovliest!
His name on yours, as erst His head on your breast.

Pray for me, Mother,—oh, pray for me now, I cry!
God only knows if it be this hour I die.

Emily Hickey

FOR THE FEAST OF ALL SAINTS

Giver of life, eternal Lord!
Thy own redeemed defend;
Mother of grace! thy children save,
And help them to the end.

* * * *

All ye who high above the stars
In heavenly glory reign!
May we through your prevailing prayers
Unto your joys attain.

Roman Breviary (translated by Edward Caswall)

"MOTHER! TO THEE MYSELF I YIELD"

Mother! to thee myself I yield,
Console me in the hour of pain;

Be thou my life's support and shield,
And by me, at my death, remain!

Anonymous (translated by Edward Caswall)

From A DESCANT UPON THE LITANY OF LORETTO

Ah, Mother! whom with many names we name,
By lore of love, which in our earthly tongue
Is all too poor, though rich love's heart of flame,
To sing thee as thou art, nor leave unsung
The greatest of the graces thou has won,
Thy chiefest excellence!
Ivory Tower! Star of the Morning! Rose
Mystical! Tower of David, our Defense!
To thee our music flows,
Who makest music for us to thy Son.
So, when the shadows come,
Laden with all contrivances of fear!
Ah, Mary! lead us home,
Through fear, through fire:
To where with faithful companies we may hear
That perfect music, which the love of God,
Who this dark way once trod,
Creates among the imperishable choir.

Lionel Johnson

AVE VERUM CORPUS NATUM

Hail, true Body born of Mary,
Which for man was crucified;
Lo! the mingled blood and water,
Flowing from the piercèd side!

Lord of Life Who once did'st suffer,
When we drew our latest breath,
Be to us our food and succour,
In the awful hour of death!

Robert Hugh Benson

TO OUR LADY

O Lady, by the stars that make
  A glory round thy head;
And by the pure uplifted hands
  That for thy children plead;
When at the Judgment-seat I stand,
  And my dread Saviour see;
When waves of night around me roll
And hell is raging for my soul—
  O then remember me.

Edward Caswall

THE LOWEST PLACE

Give me the lowest place, not that I dare
  Ask for that lowest place, but Thou hast died
That I might live and share
  Thy glory by Thy side.

Give me the lowest place; or if for me
  That lowest place too high, make one more low
Where I may sit and see
  My God and love Thee so.

Christina Rossetti

SECURITY

Outwit me, Lord, if ever hence
  This unremembering brain
Should urge these most inconstant feet
  To quit Thy side again.

Be not too sure of me though death
  Still find me at Thy side,—
Let pain, Thy soldier, break my legs
  Before I shall have died.

And when at length this heart is stopped,
 Leave not a final chance,
But send some kind centurion,
 An expert with the lance.

Charles L. O'Donnell

From VISIONS

Since, O white City! I may be,
I, a white citizen of thee:
 I claim no saint's high grace;
 Mine, but a servant's place.

I think not vainly to become
A king, who knew no martyrdom:
 Nor crown, nor palm, I crave;
 But to be Christ's poor slave.

Angels! before the Lord of lords,
Shine forth, His spiritual swords!
 Flash round the King of kings
 The snow of your white wings!

But I, too fresh from the white fire,
Humble the dreams of all desire:
 Nay! let me shine afar,
 Who am Heaven's faintest star.

Upon the eternal borders let
My still too fearful soul be set:
 There wait the Will of God,
 A loving period.

Closer I dare not come, nor see
The Face of Him, Who died for me.
 Child! thou shalt dwell apart:
 But in my Sacred Heart.

Lionel Johnson

PARAPHRASE OF PSALM 129

Out of the depths to Thee, O Lord, I cry,
Lord! gracious turn Thine ear to suppliant sigh;
If sins of man Thou scannest, who may stand
That searching eye of Thine, and chastening hand?
Oh, hear our prayers and sighs, Redeemer blest,
And grant Thy holy souls eternal rest.
And let perpetual light upon them shine;
For though not spotless, still these souls are Thine.

Anonymous

ANGEL OF THE AGONY

Jesu! by that shuddering dread which fell on Thee;
Jesu! by that cold dismay which sicken'd Thee;
Jesu! by that pang of heart which thrill'd in Thee;
Jesu! by that mount of sins which crippled Thee;
Jesu! by that sense of guilt which stifled Thee;
Jesu! by that innocence which girdled Thee;
Jesu! by that sanctity which reign'd in Thee;
Jesu! by that Godhead which was one with Thee;
Jesu! spare these souls which are so dear to Thee;
Souls, who in prison, calm and patient, wait for Thee;
Hasten, Lord, their hour, and bid them come to Thee,
To that glorious Home, where they shall gaze on Thee.

John Henry Newman

FOR THE DEAD

Help, Lord, the souls which Thou hast made,
The souls to Thee so dear,
In prison for the debt unpaid
Of sins committed here.

Those holy souls, they suffer on,
Resign'd in heart and will,

Until Thy high behest is done,
    And justice has its fill.
For daily falls, for pardon'd crime,
    They joy to undergo
The shadow of Thy cross sublime,
    The remnant of Thy woe.

Help, Lord, the souls which Thou hast made,
    The souls to Thee so dear,
In prison for the debt unpaid
    Of sins committed here.

Oh, by their patience of delay,
    Their hope amid their pain,
Their sacred zeal to burn away
    Disfigurement and stain;
Oh, by their fire of love, not less
    In keenness than the flame,
Oh, by their very helplessness,
    Oh, by Thy own great Name,
Good Jesu, help! sweet Jesu, aid
    The souls to Thee most dear,
In prison for the debt unpaid
    Of sins committed here.

John Henry Newman

POEMS OF PRAYER
ESPECIALLY FOR CHILDREN

"PRAISE THE LORD, YE CHILDREN"

Praise the Lord, ye children: praise ye the name of the Lord.

Psalm 112:1

CHILD'S MORNING HYMN

Father, we thank Thee for the night,
And for the pleasant morning light;
For rest and food and loving care
And all that makes the world so fair.

Help us to do the things we should,
To be to others kind and good;
In all we do in work and play,
To love Thee better day by day.

Rebecca J. Weston

IN THE MORNING

The morning bright
With rosy light
Has waked me from my sleep.
Father, I own
Thy love alone
Thy little one doth keep.

All through the day,
I humbly pray,
Be Thou my guard and guide.
My sins forgive,
And let me live,
Blest Jesus, near Thy side.

O make Thy rest
Within my breast,
Great Spirit of all grace;
Make me like Thee;
Then I shall be
Prepared to see Thy face.

Anonymous

FINDING YOU

Dear God, I wish I could have been
Among those girls and boys
You called to come and talk with You,
And who left all their toys,
And ran and climbed up on Your knee,
And held Your hand, and sat
Around You, learning lovely things—
I wish I had done that!
But God, I know that even now
I can get close to You.
I know You still love children—yes
Indeed! I know You do.
And so often I slip away
Into the Church and kneel
Down at the altar where You are,
And tell You all I feel.
I cannot see Your face, and yet
I know that You are there.
I know I'm just as close to You
As all those children were!

Mary Dixon Thayer

"JESUS, SEE A LITTLE CHILD"

Jesus, see a little child,
  Kneeling at his mother's knee;
Meekly pleading at Thy feet,
  Lifting up its hands to Thee.
Saviour, guide my little steps,
  Never let them halt or stray;
Wash me with Thy precious blood;
  Jesus, take my sins away!

Make me gentle, make me good,
  Let no evil fill my breast;
Never leave me night or day,
  Watch me when I play or rest.

Jesus, Saviour of the world,
  Look with pity down on me;
Though I'm but a little child,
  Teach me how to pray to Thee!

Matthias Barr

GRACE FOR A CHILD

Here a little child I stand,
Heaving up my either hand;
Cold as paddocks though they be,
Here I lift them up to Thee,
For a benison to fall
On our meat, and on us all. *Amen.*

Robert Herrick

A CHILD'S GRACE

God is great and God is good,
And we thank Him for our food.
By His hand we all are fed,
Give us, Lord, our daily bread.
Amen.

Anonymous

"LOVING JESUS, MEEK AND MILD"

Loving Jesus, meek and mild,
Look upon a little child!

Make me gentle as Thou art,
Come and live within my heart.

Take my childish hand in Thine,
Guide these little feet of mine.

So shall all my happy days
Sing their pleasant song of praise;

And the world shall always see
Christ, the holy Child, in me!

Charles Wesley

A LITTLE CHILD'S PRAYER

Make me, dear Lord, polite and kind
To everyone, I pray;
And may I ask you how you find
Yourself, dear Lord, today?

John Banister Tabb

A CHILD'S WISH

I wish I were the little key
That locks Love's Captive in,
And let Him out to go and free
A sinful heart from sin.

I wish I were the little bell
That tinkles for the Host,
When God comes down each day to dwell
With hearts He loves the most.

* * * *

But, oh! my God, I wish the most
That my poor heart may be
A home all holy for each Host
That comes in love to me.

Abram Ryan

"GENTLE JESUS, MEEK AND MILD"

Gentle Jesus, meek and mild,
Look upon a little child;

Pity my simplicity,
Suffer me to come to Thee.

Fain I would to Thee be brought;
Gracious God, forbid it not;
In the kingdom of Thy grace
Give a little child a place.

Oh supply my every want,
Feed the young and tender plant;
Day and night my keeper be,
Every moment watch o'er me.

Anonymous

PUER LOQUITUR

Lord Jesus, did it fret you so
To have to wait so long to grow?
Did you get tired of being small;
And long to be a man, and tall?

It seems to me I never can
Wait to grow up and be a man.
How could you leave your heaven to be
A little, tiny boy like me?

Edward F. Garesché

THE NEAREST FRIEND

Dear Jesus! ever at my side,
How loving Thou must be,
To leave Thy home in heaven to guard
A little child like me!

Thy beautiful and shining face
I see not, though so near;

The sweetness of Thy soft, low voice
   I am too deaf to hear.

I cannot feel Thee touch my hand
   With pressure light and mild,
To check me, as my mother did
   When I was but a child;

But I have felt Thee in my thoughts,
   Fighting with sin for me;
And when my heart loves God, I know
   The sweetness is from Thee.

Yes! when I pray, Thou prayest too;
   Thy prayer is all for me;
But when I sleep, Thou sleepest not,
   But watchest patiently.

Frederick W. Faber

A CHILD'S PRAYER
(*Ex Ore Infantium*)

Little Jesus, wast Thou shy
Once, and just as small as I?
And what did it feel like to be
Out of Heaven, and just like me?
Didst Thou sometimes think of *there,*
And ask where all the angels were?
I should think that I would cry
For my house all made of sky;
I would look about the air,
And wonder where my angels were;
And at waking 'twould distress me—
Not an angel there to dress me!

Hadst Thou ever any toys,
Like us little girls and boys?
And didst Thou play in Heaven with all
The Angels, that were not too tall,

With stars for marbles? Did the things
Play *Can you see me?* through their wings?

Didst Thou kneel at night to pray,
And didst Thou join Thy hands, this way?
And did they tire sometimes, being young,
And make the prayer seem very long?
And dost Thou like it best, that we
Should join our hands and pray to Thee?
I used to think, before I knew,
The prayer not said unless we do.
And did Thy Mother at the night
Kiss Thee and fold the clothes in right?
And didst Thou feel quite good in bed,
Kissed, and sweet, and Thy prayers said?

Thou canst not have forgotten all
That it feels like to be small:
And Thou know'st I cannot pray
To Thee in my father's way—
When Thou wast so little, say,
Could'st Thou talk Thy Father's way?—
So, a little child, come down
And hear a child's tongue like Thy own;
Take me by the hand and walk,
And listen to my baby-talk.
To Thy Father show my prayer
(He will look, Thou art so fair),
And say: "O Father, I, Thy son,
Bring the prayer of a little one."

And He will smile, that children's tongue
Has not changed since Thou wast young!

Francis Thompson

"JESUS, TENDER SHEPHERD, HEAR ME"

Jesus, tender Shepherd, hear me;
  Bless Thy little lamb tonight;

Through the darkness be Thou near me,
  Watch my sleep till morning light.

All this day Thy hand has led me,
  And I thank Thee for Thy care;
Thou hast clothed me, warmed, and fed me;
  Listen to my evening prayer.

Let my sins be all forgiven,
  Bless the friends I love so well;
Take me when I die to heaven,
  Happy there with Thee to dwell.

Mary Lundie Duncan

EVENING PRAYER

Ere on my bed my limbs I lay,
God grant me grace my prayers to say.
O God, preserve my mother dear
In strength and health for many a year;
And, oh! preserve my father too,
And may I pay him reverence due—
And may I my best thoughts employ
To be my parents' hope and joy.
And, oh! preserve my brothers both
From evil doings and from sloth;
And may we always love each other,
Our friends, our father, and our mother.
And still, O Lord, to me impart
An innocent and grateful heart,
That after my last sleep I may
Awake to Thy eternal day! Amen.

Samuel Taylor Coleridge

BEFORE SLEEPING

Matthew, Mark, Luke and John,
Bless the bed that I lie on.

Before I lay me down to sleep,
I give my soul to Christ to keep.
Four corners to my bed,
Four angels there aspread,
Two to foot and two to head,
And four to carry me when I'm dead.
I go by sea, I go by land,
The Lord made me with His right hand.
If any danger come to me,
Sweet Jesus Christ, deliver me.
He's the branch and I'm the flower,
Pray God send me a happy hour,
And if I die before I wake,
I pray that Christ my soul will take.

Anonymous—Old English Prayer

"ANGEL OF GOD, MY GUARDIAN DEAR"

Angel of God, my guardian dear,
To whom His love commits me here,
Ever this day be at my side
To light and guard, to rule and guide.

Anonymous

"NOW I LAY ME DOWN TO SLEEP"

Now I lay me down to sleep,
I pray Thee, Lord, Thy child to keep;
Thy love go with me all the night
And wake me with the morning light.

Anonymous

"MAY GOD HAVE MERCY ON US"

May God have mercy on us, and bless us: may he cause the light of his countenance to shine upon us, and may he have mercy on us.

Psalm 66:2

INDEX OF AUTHORS WITH BIOGRAPHICAL NOTES

FIELD, WILLIAM NOÉ (1915–). A priest of the Newark, N.J., archdiocese, currently on the faculty of Seton Hall University. An editor, critic and poet, 74, 128, 180

FOX, RUTH MARY (Contemporary). Born in Wisconsin, active in Wisconsin educational activities, specializing in literature, and active in Catholic poetry circles, 54, 218

FRANCIS OF ASSISI, ST. (1181–1226). Founder of the Franciscan order, one of the most universally loved saints; famous for his love of all living things, 21, 194

FRANCIS XAVIER, ST. (1506–1552). Jesuit missionary to the East Indies, and one of those who helped St. Ignatius Loyola establish the Society of Jesus, 54

GARESCHÉ, EDWARD F. (1876–1960). A Jesuit, founder of The Queen's Work (St. Louis, Mo.), active in sodality and missionary work and in the Catholic Medical Missionary Board. A prolific writer, including meditations and poetry, 76, 143, 261

GILBERT, ELLEN (Contemporary U.S.). No data available, 130

GILMORE, FLORENCE (Contemporary U.S.). A writer of prose as well as of poetry, 55

GILTINAN, CAROLINE (Mrs. Leo P. Harlow) (1884–). Engaged in medical work during World War I, then with the Hoover Relief Administration, and the Associated Press. A frequent contributor of verse to periodicals and active in poetry circles, 158

GRAY, JOHN (1866–1934). Ordained to the priesthood in 1901, and later became rector of St. Peter's Church, Edinburgh, Scotland, 53

GREGORY THE GREAT, POPE, ST. (538–594). Benedictine monk who became Pope, initiated reforms in monasticism and made enduring changes in the papal system, 161, 188

GREGORY NAZIANZEN, ST. (ca. 329–389). Bishop, opponent of Arianism and one of the Doctors of the Church, 161, 164

GRIFFIN, GERALD (1803–1840). Irish novelist, dramatist and poet, 132

GUINEY, LOUISE IMOGEN (1861–1920). American Catholic poet and essayist who spent most of her adult life in England, 231

GUYON, MADAME (Jeanne Marie Bouvier de la Motte) (1648–1717). French mystic, 23, 79

HART, HOWARD (Contemporary U.S.). Dramatist and poet, 175

JOHN OF THE CROSS, ST. (1549–1591). Spanish mystic and religious reformer, founder, with St. Teresa of Avila, of the order of Discalced Carmelites, 52

JOHNSON, LIONEL (1867–1902). English convert to Catholicism, whose early death left his great poetic promise unfulfilled, 101, 214, 215, 251, 253

JOHNSON, VICTORIA SAFFELLE (Contemporary). A Librarian at the Pacific School of Religion, Berkeley, California, a poet, hymnologist, and anthologist, 71

JONSON, BEN (1573–1637). English playwright, poet and friend of Shakespeare, Herrick and other noted writers of the period, 122

KAHN, HELEN R. (Contemporary U.S.). No other data available, 138

KEITH, JOSEPH JOEL (1908–). Prolific American poet who has contributed to leading American quality magazines and to journals of similar standing in England, Italy, India, etc. He has made recordings of his poetry for the Library of Congress, Harvard University and other colleges. Eight volumes of his poems have been published, 128

KELLY, BLANCHE MARY (1881–). For many years on the faculty of the College of Mount St. Vincent, New York, now professor emeritus; author of many poems, 48, 207

KEN, THOMAS (1637–1711). English clergyman and hymn writer, 105

KILMER, ALINE (1888–1941). Widow of Joyce Kilmer; many believe her poetry superior to her better-known husband's, 125, 209

KILMER, JOYCE (1886–1918). Gallant and likeable American poet, critic, editor; famous for his poem "Trees." He was killed in action in France during World War I, 2, 124

LANKFORD, FRANCES STOAKLEY (Contemporary U.S.). No other data available, 172, 203, 208

LAUBE, CLIFFORD J. (Contemporary). Twenty-four years on the *N.Y. Times,* retired in 1953 as its national news editor. President of the Catholic Poetry Society of America 1955–1961, currently poetry editor of two periodicals, and founder and head of the Monastine Press, specializing in volumes of Catholic poetry, 101

LEARY, ELEANOR M. (Contemporary U.S.). No other data available, 170

LINGARD, JOHN (1771–1851). English priest and historian, 131

the first president of the Catholic Poetry Society of America, 72, 179, 217, 252

PALEN, JENNIE M. (Contemporary). American poet, 75

PARSONS, ERNESTINE (Contemporary U.S.). No other data available, 138

PETER DAMIAN, ST. (1007–1072). A Benedictine, a Cardinal, and a Doctor of the Church, 245

PICO DELLA MIRANDOLA, GIOVANNI FRANCESCO, COUNT (1463–1494). Italian humanist, philosopher and author; known for his neo-Platonic studies and work in Hebrew philosophy, 125

POPE, ALEXANDER (1688–1744). English poet famous for his satire, wit, invective and the technical perfection of his art, 90, 107

POSTGATE, VENERABLE NICHOLAS (1596–1679). English priest, educated at Douay, returned to England as a missionary, captured and executed because of his Faith, 72

POWERS, JESSICA (Contemporary). The writing name of Sister Miriam of the Holy Spirit, prioress of a community of Discalced Carmelite nuns in Wisconsin, and author of a series of volumes of superior poetry, 2, 181, 182

PRATI, GIOVANNI (1815–1884). Italian poet, 249

PROCTER, ADELAIDE ANNE (1825–1864). English poet; daughter of Barry Cornwall (pseudonym of Bryan Waller Procter, who was a poet and friend of Dickens and other literary figures), 100, 152, 165, 173, 190, 195, 232

QUARLES, FRANCIS (1592–1644). English religious poet, has been compared to George Herbert in his choice of imagery from everyday life, 56, 70, 86, 104

RANDALL, JAMES RYDER (1839–1908). American journalist and poet, noted for his "Maryland, My Maryland," 93

RAWES, HENRY A. (1826–1885). English convert to Catholicism, educator, superior of the Oblate Fathers, well-known preacher and writer, 96

ROLLE, RICHARD (ca. 1300–1349). English recluse who wrote religious treatises and poems, 224

ROONEY, JOHN JEROME (1866–1934). Resident of New York City, for years a judge on the N.Y. State Court of Claims, and a poet, 96, 198

ROSSETTI, CHRISTINA (1830–1894). English poet of Italian descent, sister of D. G. and W. M. Rossetti, and devout Anglican. Her poetry is noted for its religious intensity and technical finish, 55, 85, 114, 123, 184, 197, 219, 234, 252

RYAN, ABRAM (1839–1886). Catholic chaplain with Southern armies during the Civil War, famous for his post-Civil War poem "The Conquered Banner," 260

SANTEUL, JEAN BAPTISTE DE, S. J. (1630–1697). Great classical poet, 61

SCOTT, SIR WALTER (1771–1832). Famous Scottish novelist, poet, historian, and biographer, 192

SHILLITO, EDWARD (1872–1948). An English clergyman who wrote a great deal of poetry, 94

SISTER M. MADELEVA (1887–). A member of the Sisters of the Congregation of Holy Cross, professor of English and head of the English Department of St. Mary's College, Notre Dame, Indiana, 1914–1919; President of St. Mary's College 1934–1961. One of the best-known and admired American Catholic poets; recipient of many honors and awards, 158

SISTER MARCELA DE CARPIO (1605–1688). A Spanish nun and poet, 46, 51

SISTER MARIS STELLA (1899–). A member of the Sisters of St. Joseph, born in Iowa, chairman of the English Department of the College of St. Catherine, St. Paul, Minn., 213

SISTER MARY ADA (Contemporary U.S.). A member of the Sisters of St. Joseph, 233

SISTER MARY ANGELITA (1878–). A member of the Sisters of Charity of the Blessed Virgin Mary, Dubuque, Iowa, 147

SISTER MARY DAVIDA (Contemporary U.S.). A member of the Sisters of the Immaculate Heart of Mary, 76

SISTER MARY MAURA (1916–). A member of the School Sisters of Notre Dame, recognized as one of the finest contemporary Catholic poets; on the faculty of the College of Notre Dame of Maryland, in Baltimore, 127, 179, 206

SISTER MARY PAULINUS (Contemporary U.S.). A member of the Sisters of the Immaculate Heart of Mary, 79

SISTER MIRIAM, R.S.M. (Contemporary U.S.). A member of the Sisters of Mercy, for many years on the English faculty of College of Misericordia, Dallas, Pa., 63, 146

SPALDING, JOHN LANCASTER (1840–1916). Kentucky-born, Catholic bishop of Peoria, Illinois. A writer and lecturer of great learning, eloquence and influence, 56, 59, 103, 109, 116, 184

SPENSER, EDMUND (1553–1598). English poet of great skill and enduring fame, 60

STANYHURST, RICHARD (1547–1618). Irish author and translator, 225

STODDARD, CHARLES WARREN (1843–1909). American traveler and author, 229

STRAHAN, SPEER (1898–1959). Originally a member of the Holy Cross Fathers, Notre Dame, Indiana. He became a diocesan priest in Michigan and taught at the Catholic University of America, 153

SULLIVAN, A. M. (Contemporary U.S.). N.Y.C. business executive and associate editor of *Spirit,* his spiritually-oriented poetry has earned increasing recognition, 100, 140

TABB, JOHN BANISTER (1845–1909). A Virginian, convert to Catholicism in 1872, ordained for priesthood in 1884; teacher and poet who lost his sight in his later years, 2, 20, 30, 50, 64, 102, 167, 246, 247, 259

TERESA OF AVILA, ST. (1515–1582). Carmelite nun, mystic and religious superior of great ability, 46, 54, 247, 248

THAYER, MARY DIXON (1897–). Wife of a Boston physician, her religious poetry has long been popular, 74, 87, 146, 258

THOMPSON, FRANCIS (1860–1907). English poet, known for his mystical religious poetry, especially "The Hound of Heaven." His addiction to opium, resulting degradation and, finally, rehabilitation is as well-known as his poetry, 170, 263

THORNTON, FRANCIS BEAUCHESNE (Contemporary U.S.). A priest of the St. Paul, Minn., diocese, editor of the Catholic Digest Book Club, occasional lecturer, author of some sixteen volumes of biography, criticism, history and poetry; most recently of *This is The Rosary,* published by Hawthorn Books, Inc., in 1961, 41

TOBIN, JAMES EDWARD (Contemporary U.S.). Former newspaperman, member of the faculty of Fordham University, currently professor in English department of Queens College, New York, on editorial board of The Catholic Book Club, anthologist, associate editor of *Spirit,* and a poet, 220

TREGIAN, FRANCIS (1548–1608). English Roman Catholic who lost favor with Queen Elizabeth I of England when he rejected

INDEX OF TITLES

INDEX OF FIRST LINES

THE AUTHOR AND HIS BOOK

Ralph L. Woods *was born in St. Louis, Missouri in 1904. For many years he worked for the Sinclair Oil Company, then left to write full-time. In 1948 he joined the N.A.M. as staff writer. After five years he returned to full-time, free-lance writing and anthologizing, interrupted by several periods as a consulting editor for the* Catholic Digest. *He has written numerous articles for* The Saturday Review, The Critic, Catholic Digest, The Sign, American Legion Magazine, The Freeman *and others. Mr. Woods lives with his wife, Lillias, in Ramsey, New Jersey. He is the author of* America Reborn: A Plan for Decentralization of Industry (*Longmans Green, 1939*), Pilgrim Places in North America (*Longmans Green, 1939*), A Treasury of the Familiar (*Macmillan, 1942*), Behold the Man (*Macmillan, 1944*), The World of Dreams (*Random, 1947*), A Second Treasury of the Familiar (*Macmillan, 1950*), A Treasury of Inspiration (*Crowell, 1951*), The Businessman's Book of Quotations (*McGraw-Hill, 1953*), A Treasury of Catholic Thinking (*Crowell, 1953*), The Consolations of Catholicism (*Appleton Century, 1954*), The Catholic Companion to the Bible (*Lippincott, 1956*), A Treasury of the Dog (*Putnam, 1956*), A Treasury of Friendship (*McKay, 1957*), The Catholic Concept of Love and Marriage (*Lippincott, 1958*), The Family Reader of American Masterpieces (*Crowell, 1959*), *and* Famous Poems and the Little-Known Stories Behind Them (*Hawthorn, 1961*).

Poems of Prayer (*Hawthorn, 1962*) *was completely manufactured by American Book–Stratford Press, Inc., New York, N.Y. The body type is Fairfield, which was designed for the linotype by Rudolph Ruzicka in 1939.*

A HAWTHORN BOOK